The Art Of

Seeing Double Or Better

In Business

(How All Of Us Can Be More Innovative)

Ernie J. Zelinski

VIP BOOKS

Visions **I**nternational **P**ublishing

Vancouver, B.C., Canada

VIP BOOKS Edition

Published by Visions International Publishing,
Vancouver, B.C., Canada

First printing September, 1989 by Art Design Printing
Inc., Edmonton, Alberta, Canada

Canadian Cataloguing in Publication Data

Zelinski, Ernie J. (Ernie John), 1949-

   The art of seeing double or better in business

ISBN 0-9694194-0-6

1. Creative ability in business. I. Title .

HD53.Z44 1989   650.1   C89-091565-2

To all the creative people throughout the ages who have been willing to risk, be different, challenge the status quo, ruffle a few feathers, and in the process truly make a big difference in this world.

Also to my mother who allowed me to have my independence in my early years. This gave me the freedom to discover the creative process.

Acknowledgements

With special thanks to:

- Ron Moore of George's Cycle for hiring me to conduct my first company seminar on creativity.
- Patricia Murray in Vancouver for reading the manuscript and for your valuable editorial comments.
- Catherine Williams of Travel Care for your comments and inspiration in having me complete publication of this book.
- Dan and Laura O'Brien for your wonderful words of support on my trips to Vancouver.
- Jim Egler of Carleton University in Ottawa for assisting me in creative loafing at the High Level Diner.
- Bill Comrie of The Brick Warehouse for taking the time to read the manuscript and offer your comments.
- Henry and Diana Dembicki for your support and advice as well as the delicious meals.
- Zoria Crilly and Pat Craig of the U of A Faculty of Extension for reading the manuscript and offering your kind words.
- Laurie Johnston of the Good Samaritan Care Centre for taking the time to do some of the illustrations.
- Also to Ann Nixon of Alberta Speakers Bureau, Ross Bradford of the U or A Faculty of Business, Hugh Nicholson of McMan Youth Services Assn., Tricia Cisakowski of U of A Research Services, Carol Ann Probert of Alta. Assn. of Services for Children and Families, Brad Harper of AGT, and Norma Gutteridge of U of A Press for reading the manuscript and providing your individual comments.

PREFACE - THE PARADOX OF CREATIVITY

This book is about how to enhance your creativity. How do I know that your creativity has to be enhanced? I don't; however, I have made a few interesting observations over the last few years while teaching creativity. A strange paradox is evident; the people and organizations who most need to have their creative abilities enhanced are the most resistant to participating in any related learning activities.

The opposite is true with creative people and innovative companies. They are most eager to look at new ways and not-so-new ways to stimulate their creativity. A good example is Grant Lovig and his staff at Company's Coming Publishing. They helped Grant's mother, Jean Paré, market over 4,000,000 of her "Company's Coming" cookbooks in an industry where 5000 is considered a bestseller. With their phenomenal success in innovative marketing, the staff at Company's Coming are one of the last groups I know which need a lesson in creativity and innovation. Nevertheless, Grant and his staff were most receptive to a creativity seminar I conducted for them.

Many people and companies need to know more about how to be more innovative. They could benefit immensely from improving their creative thinking. There is a Catch-22; because they don't understand the benefits of creativity, they will never take steps to learn about it. Of course, they will never understand the benefits until they take steps to learn about it.

Why do the highly-creative individuals of this world spend time on enhancing their creativity? The enhancement of creativity is like most self-improvement activities. Self-improvement is not a destination; it is a journey. Even creative people in this world have to practice and remind themselves what makes people creative and successful. The thing that separates successful people from the less successful ones is that the successful people are always taking part in interesting journeys of learning. They are doers. They continually strive for self-improvement. The less successful are not doers. They may be interested in destinations but resist making the necessary journeys. Without journeys come no new destinations.

The journey of learning helps us get to new and exciting places. My wish is that all participants in my seminars and readers of my books find themselves on a worthwhile journey. I hope it is like the wonderful one I have had in learning about creativity and teaching it to others. Bon voyage.

Ernie J. Zelinski

TABLE OF CONTENTS

INTRODUCTION

Introduction To Creativity And Innovation

"The company's most urgent task then is .... innovation from everyone."

- Tom Peters, author of "Thriving On Chaos"

"Some men see things as they are and ask, "Why?" I see them as they have never been and ask, "Why not?"

George Bernard Shaw

CREATIVITY IN BUSINESS

Creativity is increasingly valued by business organizations; many are making it one of their highest training priorities. Business Week reports that over half of the Fortune 500 Companies send their chief executives as well as other important employees for creativity training.

Why is there this interest in creativity training? Companies have found that the area of creativity was not well taught by the school systems. Most, but not all, school systems still dispense an education that teaches students to deal only with the linear, logical, and rational picture of life. Today this is not enough. In an age of uncertainty, we must be able to deal with the whole picture. This demands that we must feel at home with the nonanalytical, intuitive, and experiential side of life.

The emphasis of creativity in business is a recent phenomenon. In the past creativity was thought to exist in the realm of the artist and musician and not in the realm of the business person. With innovation being cited as one of the three most important factors for today's business success (along with customer service and employee leadership), creativity has been given more attention by companies. Innovative thinking is important for the success of both individuals and organizations. In a world which is changing at a unprecedented rate, ingenuity is needed to respond to the unexpected. The generation of new initiatives is what creativity in business is all about.

Educational institutions are also seeing a need for teaching creativity. Creativity is showing up in programs right from kindergarden up to graduate programs at universities. For example, the Graduate School of Business at Stanford University has a course in personal creativity.

"In the new corporation, creativity and individuality are organizational treasures."

- John Nasbitt, Megatrends

"Innovating - creating new products, new services, new ways of turning out goods more cheaply - has become the most urgent concern of corporations everywhere."

- Fortune Magazine, Cover Story, June 6, 1988

The importance of being creative in today's world cannot be overemphasized. Paul Torrence, an expert in creativity, states:

"The genius of the future will be the creative mind adapting itself to the shape of things to come......The skills of creative thinking must be recognized as mankind's most important adaptability skills. Such skills must become basic to the curriculum of schools, homes, business, and other agencies."

Tom Peters, in his recent book, *"Thriving On Chaos"*, argues that the successful people in the immediate future will be those who are flexible thinkers and love change. The successful corporations will be the constantly innovating ones. These organizations will not only quickly adapt to shifting circumstances, but will also take advantage of them by being innovative.

Business people, educators and government leaders are now more aware of the benefits of creativity. Creativity is the corporation's competitive edge in today's rapidly changing world. It is the special talent that develops the right market segment. It is the ability that turns a crisis into an opportunity. It is the insight that recognizes a better and cheaper way to produce the company's existing product. It is innovation that helps a business prosper, while others fail.

Exercise - You And Creativity

1. Give a brief definition of creativity.

2. When was the last time when you were creative? How?

.... Today

.... Yesterday

.... Last week

.... Last month or before

3. What motivates you to be creative? What principles do you consider important for becoming more creative?

CREATIVITY IS -
HAVING YOUR CAKE AND EATING IT TOO

Just what is creativity? Posing this question to others always results in a number of interesting definitions. Here are some answers typical of those that I receive from the participants in my seminars.

Creativity is being different.

Creativity is the Mona Lisa.

Creativity is thinking differently.

Creativity is being a genius.

Creativity is having your cake and eating it too.

Creativity is being able to solve problems.

Creativity is something children are good at.

Creativity is playing a prank on a friend.

Creativity is being unreasonable and crazy.

Creativity is daydreaming at work without being caught.

Creativity is being able to generate many options to just about anything.

Creativity is the ability to enjoy everything in life.

These are just a few of the many different definitions that are possible for creativity. All of the definitions represent some essence of the creative process. Even "creativity is being a genius" is appropriate since we all have some genius in us. The point is that creativity means different things to different people. Creativity is an experience and all our experiences are somewhat different. The myriad of definitions reflects the many sides of what being creative is all about.

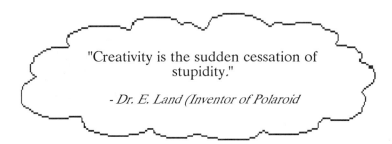

"Creativity is the sudden cessation of stupidity."

- Dr. E. Land (Inventor of Polaroid

My personal definition of creativity is that creativity is "the art of seeing double or better". Seeing double or better refers to the ability to see more than one solution to just about anything. Being creative is being able to see or imagine a great deal of opportunity to life's problems. Creativity is having many options. This book is about how to enhance our ability to generate opportunity and options that we would not otherwise generate.

In assigning a general definition to creativity, we can say that creativity is the ability to think or do something new. By new we do not mean new to all the world. We mean new to the person who is thinking or doing it. The ability to come up with something new is generally not a function of heredity nor is it a function of an extremely high education.

There is no magic associated with the skill of creativity. The ability to see more and come up with new ideas or solutions can be learned. Creativity is a skill that can be developed by just about everyone. It is a thinking skill, not difficult to master. But no matter what our level of mastery, it will remain a skill that we can always improve. All being creative involves is first being aware of some basic techniques and then using these techniques in our lives. There are many benefits to be gained by both organizations and individuals from practicing creativity. The benefits are listed on the following page.

Page 8 lists the seventeen principles that I consider basic for being creative in business. The principles can be applied to personal matters as well as business.

There is no claim here that these are the only available principles for enhancing your creativity. Other principles and techniques exist. The objective is to enhance your ability to see and generate more options by using as many techniques as possible.

The ultimate objective is to help you discover the genius within you. Then you can have your cake and eat it to. How? Just get yourself two cakes.

BENEFITS FROM ENHANCING CREATIVITY & INNOVATION

Benefits To Organizations

☆ Fresh ideas for more solutions

☆ More quality in ideas and solutions

☆ Improved decision making

☆ Increased effectiveness

☆ Productivity increases

☆ Generation of new business opportunites

☆ Superior business performance

Benefits To Employees

☆ Personal growth

☆ More ability in decision making

☆ More enthusiasm for solving problems

☆ Increased confidence to deal with new and bigger challenges

☆ Different perspectives toward work and personal life

☆ Improved skills in management

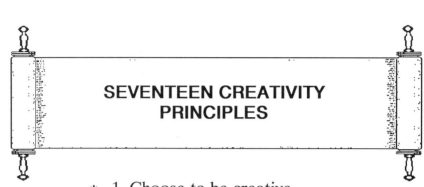

SEVENTEEN CREATIVITY PRINCIPLES

* 1. Choose to be creative
* 2. Look for many solutions
* 3. Write your ideas down
* 4. Fully analyze your ideas
* 5. Define your goal
* 6. See problems as opportunities
* 7. Look for the obvious
* 8. Take risks
* 9. Dare to be different
* 10. Be unreasonable
* 11. Have fun and be foolish
* 12. Be spontaneous
* 13. Be in the now
* 14. Practice lateral thinking
* 15. Challenge rules & assumptions
* 16. Delay your decision
* 17. Be persistent

CHAPTER 1

How To Be Creative And Write Graffiti

I hate graffiti

So do I, in fact I hate all Italian Food

-Graffiti in the washroom

"Imagination is more important than knowledge"

- Albert Einstein

CREATIVITY THROUGH THE AGES

Let us begin this chapter with the following two exercises

Exercise #1-1 - Columbus And The Eggheads

At the Royal Court in Spain, Christopher Columbus asked the assistants if they could get an egg to stand on its end. They tried and could not do it. They thought it was impossible.

Columbus then said he could do it. The assistants bet him he could not. Columbus then proceeded to make the egg stand on its end. He collected his bet much to the frustration of the assistants.

What do you think Columbus did?

Exercise #1-2 - Creativity And Tardy Employees

The manager of a marketing department of a large corporation had a problem. Starting time was 8:00 o'clock. One of his employees was constantly late by about 30 minutes. She was the most creative and productive employee in the company.

The manager came up with a unique way of solving the problem.

How would you have solved the problem of the tardy employee?

CREATIVITY AND KNOWLEDGE

Without any prior knowledge of what either Columbus or the Manager had done, did you generate some good new ideas for solving each exercise? Were there new thoughts in your solutions or were you searching for something that you already know? Keep this in mind. Creativity goes beyond what you already know. What you know is just knowledge.

Creating a disturbance! Not guilty, Your Honour. I know I am not creative.

Knowledge is not creativity. Creativity transcends knowledge. This is an important distinction. Many people feel that grasping and remembering a myriad of facts and figures will give them the edge in life. This may give them the edge in trivial pursuits; however, having the edge in the important things in life is dependent on having the creative edge. The ability to think in new ways is much more important than the ability to remember what team won the Stanley Cup or which Fortune 500 company had the highest profits last year.

We have broadly defined creativity as the ability to come up with something new. How new were your ideas on how to stand an egg on its end or how to deal with a tardy employee? Knowledge of old ways is valuable; nevertheless, we must often look for fresh ideas if we are to find more effective solutions. Innovative thinking is approaching life's situations and problems in new ways so that these situations and problems are handled with greater ease.

New approachs are possible for just about anything. Abraham Maslow stated that a truly good soup can be as creative as a great painting or a marvelous symphony. Creativity can be found in music, painting, cooking, engineering, carpentry, accounting, law, economics, leisure and sports. It has been with us through the ages and will continue to play an even more important role in our future development.

Creativity can be found in every endeavour in human life. Here are some examples of creativity:

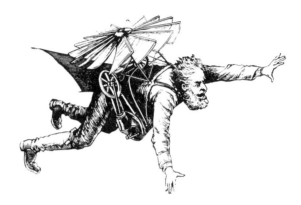

Creativity is standing an egg on its edge.
Creativity is getting a tardy person to be early.
Creativity is wanting to know.
Creativity is cooking a new dish.
Creativity is finding a faster route home.
Creativity is developing a new product.
Creativity is providing a new service.
Creativity is writing a book.
Creativity is finding a solution on the computer.
Creativity is living happily while unemployed.
Creativity is planning an exotic vacation.
Creativity is writing graffiti in the washroom.

Creativity is all of the above and much more. From these examples to the lawyer's creativity and the graffiti on the following pages to the examples cited in subsequent chapters, creativity is endless. Creativity can be applied to just about any task in any personal or business situation.

EVEN LAWYERS CAN BE CREATIVE

The true account of the court action described below shows that lawyers, like everyone else, can be very creative.

On November 23, 1917 a Statement Of Claim was filed in the District Court Of Battleford by the plaintiffs, H. C. Humphrey and H. G. Chard, for damages to their female pig allegedly caused by a male pig owned by the defendant, Joseph Odishaw. The Statement of Claim, in part, read:

"That on or about the 4th day of November, 1917, a boar, the property of the defendant, was allowed by the Defendant to run at large contrary to the provisions of the said By-Law and the said boar broke and entered the lands of the Plaintiffs, being the lands above described, on or about the 4th day of November, 1917 and served a valuable sow of the Plaintiffs and the said sow became in pig to the great damage of the Plaintiffs.

The Plaintiffs therefore claim: $200.00 damages, and the cost of this action."

On January 14, 1918, the defendant's lawyer, A.M. Panton K.C., of the City of North Battleford filed a Statement of Defence. The third alternative in the Statement of Defence reads:

"In the alternative the Defendant says if his boar entered the close of the plaintiffs and had intercourse with the said sow that he did so at the solicitation of the said sow and that the said boar merely yielded to her blandishments and that she was solely guilty of the behaviour complained of or is at least in "pari delicto" with the said boar and that her masters the said plaintiffs are guilty of an offence against the public morals in keeping a sow of such depraved habits to corrupt the morals of the neighborhood.

The Defendant waives his right to a counter-claim against the plaintiffs for lowering the vital powers of the said boar upon which the defendant might properly look for sustenance.

The Defendant therefore claims that this action be dismissed against him with costs."

Incidently, there was no record of a trial or judgment in this case. Apparently the case was dropped or dismissed.

CREATIVITY PUT IN A CAN

(The Creativity Of Good Graffiti)

Isaac Newton was right!
This is the center of Graffiti

Down with gravity

Bad spellers of the world,
Untie!

Jesus saves!
(but Gretzky tips in the rebound)

I'd give my left arm to be
ambidextrous

Reality is for those who cannot handle booze or drugs

Sex education is interesting but
I never get any homework

POINT OF VIEW IS
RELATIVE
(Said Picasso to Einstein)

PREPARE TO MEET GOD!
(Jacket and tie, no jeans)

PLEASE DO NOT FLUSH
WHILE TRAIN IS IN STATION
(Except in Hamilton)

Repeal the law of gravity

Roy Rogers was trigger
happy

Power corrupts. Absolute power is even more fun.

I'M SCHIZOPHRENIC
(So am I. That makes four of us)

I can't stand intolerance

The DC-10 is not what it is cracked up to be

THE WORLD WILL END AT MIDNIGHT TONIGHT!
(12:30 in Newfoundland)

BE ALERT!
Your country needs lerts

My dad says they don't work
(written on contraceptive vending machine)

BILL STICKERS WILL BE PROSECUTED
(Bill Stickers is innocent. OK!)

Celibacy is not an inherited characteristic

Drink wet cement and get really stoned

Eve was framed

We should hang all the extremists!

God is dead.
-Nietzsche
Nietzsche is dead.
-God

Death is natures way of telling you to slow down

DON'T LOOK UP HERE! THE JOKE IS IN YOUR HANDS!
(written above a urinal)

STALIN'S GRAVE IS A COMMUNIST PLOT

Graffiti's days are numbered. The writing is on the wall

WORSE CHEWING GUM I HAVE EVER TASTED
(written on contraceptive vending machine)
(added) I agree, but, Oh! what bubbles!

Humpty Dumpty was pushed

Peals of laughter
Screams of joy
I was here before Kilroy

Shut your mouth
Shut your face
Kilroy built the ruddy place

THE CREATIVE WAY

Creative thinking can be broken down into two types. Both types are important for the creative process.

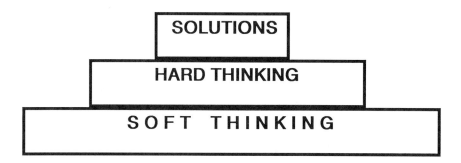

Soft Thinking - is the mode of thinking that most of us can improve on. This is the thinking that many artists and mucisians are good at. School systems and organizations normally frown at us if we think softly.

Soft thinking requires us to be flexible and random. It involves the unreasonable and the nonjudgmental. Humour and playfulness originate from soft thinking. This mode of thinking is valuable for generating a large number of ideas. Researchers say it is performed by the right side of our brains. Soft thinking should be done before any hard thinking is started.

Hard Thinking - is the type of thinking that most of us are pretty good at. It is the thinking that the school systems emphasize and reward us for. Organizations reward us highly for this type of thinking as well.

This thinking mode makes us logical and practical. It is what our parents want us to be. Society, as well, prefers us when we are logical and practical.

Hard thinking is needed for analysis of ideas. This is where we focus on useable solutions to our problems. We use hard thinking to put our plan into action. The left part of the brain is responsible for this thinking mode.

Solutions - require the two thinking processes for them to have both quality and quantity. The problem is that most of us don't use both styles of thinking effectively. Many of us use mainly the hard-thinking process whereas some of us utilize mainly the soft-thinking process.

Innovative solutions are dependent on both modes of thinking. First we should generate many ideas using soft thinking. Then, using hard thinking processes, we should evaluate the ideas for their merits. Our end result should be several good options for the problem in question.

True creative thinking is a balance of soft and hard thinking, both used at appropriate times. Problem solving mainly through hard-thinking is not effective if there are few ideas with which to work. Similarly, it is not effective to have generated a lot of ideas via soft thinking and not have properly analyzed and implemented these ideas.

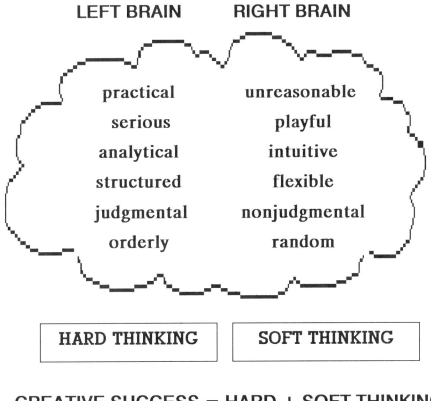

LEFT BRAIN   **RIGHT BRAIN**

practical	unreasonable
serious	playful
analytical	intuitive
structured	flexible
judgmental	nonjudgmental
orderly	random

HARD THINKING   **SOFT THINKING**

CREATIVE SUCCESS = HARD + SOFT THINKING

Chapter 1 Notes

Exercises

#1-1

Columbus went into the kitchen and boiled the egg. Then he smashed the end of the egg on the table, causing the egg to stand on its end.

Note there are many other ways to stand an egg on its end. In my seminars we have come up with at least 20.

#2-1

The manager gave the employee the only key to the office and made this employee in charge of seeing everyone else was on time.

Of course this problem has many solutions.

CHAPTER 2

Robbed Blind By The Creativity Bandits

"... modern education which stresses logic, seems to squelch creativity"

- Business Week, Cover Story, September, 1985

"I never let my schooling interfere with my education"

- Mark Twain

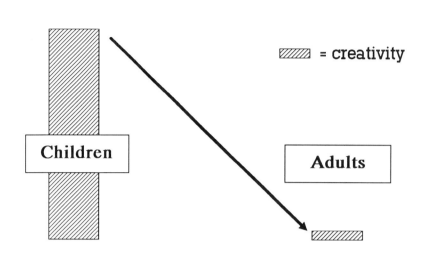

THE CREATIVITY BANDITS

Adults often wonder why young children can have as much fun with the cardboard box that a toy came in as with the toy itself. The answer is simple. Children are just more creative than adults. Most adults have become too structured in their thinking, especially towards having fun. They could not imagine there are so many interesting ways to enjoy a cardboard box.

Researchers confirm that children are much more creative than adults. What has happened to the creative abilities during those years in between childhood and adulthood? Obviously we encounter many walls to expressing our creativity in the world around us.

In fact it is worse than that. These walls act more like bandits than just barriers. By the time we are in mid adulthood, nearly all of the creativity we had as children has been taken away by these culprits. Business Week, in their September 30, 1985 cover story on business creativity, reported that an adult of 40 is about 2% as creative as a child of 5.

Who are the responsible culprits who rob us blind of 98% of our creativity by the time we are 40 years old? Who can we blame?

The following exercise may give some clues.

Exercise #2-1 - To Logo Or Not To Logo

You are the new Assistant Manager of the Marketing Department of a fairly large company, Trane Computer Systems Ltd. Your boss, the General Manager of Marketing, has just come into your office and announced that the company wants to project a new image. She has asked you to personally design a new logo for the company. This new logo has to be done within two weeks.

You realize that the assistant marketing manager before you was a commercial artist who did all the important art work for promotions. You believe your background in art leaves a lot to be desired. All you know about art is what you took in elementary school. You have not done anything relating to art since. No one else in your department claims any more art ability than you do.

How would you respond to this task?

What did you choose to do in the above exercise? Did you give some thought to designing the logo yourself? If you did not, think why you chose to avoid the task. It could be due to those creativity bandits having robbed you of your willingness to undertake challenging and creative tasks.

There are four main bandits.

THE FOUR MAIN BANDITS

☆ 1. Society

☆ 2. Educational Institutions

☆ 3. Organizations

☆ 4. Ourselves

THE SOCIETAL BANDITS

> Conformity is the jailer of freedom and the enemy of growth.
> - *John F. Kennedy, UN*

> Nature only makes dumb animals. We owe the fools to society
> - *Honore De Balzac*

If you decided to avoid designing the logo because you have no training in commercial art, you have allowed yourself to be a victim of societal programming. Cultural programming influences us to think that we have to possess a degree or formal training in a certain field to be able to accomplish anything worthwhile in that field. This thinking is absurd. Let us look at a few examples of the many people who accomplished things in fields in which they had no formal training.

☆ The *Coca-Cola*® logo was designed by an accountant with no training in artwork.

☆ Eli Whitney, a school teacher, invented the cotton gin.

☆ Samuel Morse, an artist, invented the telegraph.

☆ Werner Erhard, with no formal training in pyschology, put together one of the most successful human potential seminars ever.

☆ Robert Campeau, a grade eight dropout, amassed a billion dollar department store empire.

Society's pressure to conform to its programming takes many forms and has many effects. Cultural taboos and tradition are followed to the detriment of new ideas. An over-emphasis on competition results in people doing things they would not otherwise do. Similarly an over-emphasis on cooperation results in group think. Reason and logic are considered appropriate. Humor, intuition, and fantasy are not appreciated. All of these societal factors rob us of opportunities to be creative.

THE EDUCATIONAL BANDITS

> In the first place God made idiots.That was for practice. Then he made Schoolboards.
> *- Mark Twain*

> Education is very admirable but let us not forget that anything worth knowing cannot be taught.
> *- Oscar Wilde*

☆ Someone once asked the late inventor and philosopher, Buckminister Fuller, how he came to be such a genius. He replied that he was not a genius. He stated that he had just not been as damaged by the school system as a lot of other people. He felt that the school system can damage us in many ways.

☆ Fred Smith who started the highly successful courier service, Federal Express, wrote a paper about the business before he started it. His professor did not think too highly of the idea and gave him a low mark in the paper. Fortunately Fred Smith was not influenced by the over-intellectual assessment by the professor. His company is now one of the biggest and most innovative courier firms in the world.

You may have chosen not to design the logo in Exercise #2-1 because you would not know the right way of going about it. Schools teaching us to look for the right way or the one "right" answer is an educational shortcoming. There are many right ways of designing logos as there are many answers to most problems. People leave school systems thinking there is a formula for everything when in fact the majority of business problems cannot be solved with formulas. More creative ways are needed.

In most school systems reason and logic are over taught at the expense of other important matters. What the school systems ignore is that business decision making in today's world relies not only on reason and logic. Executive officers report using intuition in at least 40% of their major decisions. Yet consideration for the intuitive is absent from most school programs. So are other creativity factors of vision, humor, and enthusiasm.

ORGANIZATIONAL BANDITS

A lot of companies say they are innovative and supportive of creative people. Few really are. Saying the company is innovative sounds nice. These companies say they are innovative because this is the thing to say in this day and age. Looking at many companies' actions reveals a different story. The actions look more like an unconscious attempt to vandalize the creativity shown by the most innovative employees of the organization.

Most of us would not attempt to design the logo in the situation represented in Exercise #2-1 because of organizational factors which discourage creative attempts. Being creative involves risk taking. Risk taking is often something we avoid at work. The potential consequences scare us.

When a highly-creative employee shows up at a company, the company will often not support the person being highly creative. Highly- innovative people question tradition, challenge the rules, suggest new ways of doing things, tell the truth about things and appear disruptive to the rest of the employees. The qualities that make these people innovative are usually frowned upon by the company. Attempts are made to transform them to being like the rest of the group.

Group norms are protected at the expense of individual effort and ingenuity. Autocratic bosses discourage initiative. The organization sacrifices innovation and creativity to maintain a comfort level so it does not have to deal with the discomfort and disruptiveness neccessary for innovation.

Although today's corporations need innovative employees to be highly successful, a lot of organizations end up robbing their employees of the opportunity to be innovative. Success eludes these organizations in the end.

THE SELF BANDITS

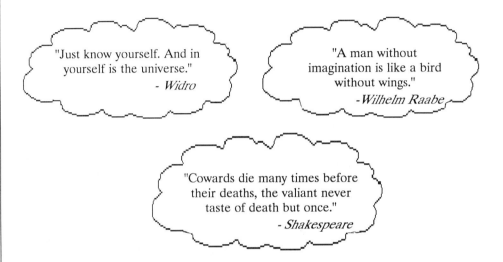

"Just know yourself. And in yourself is the universe."
- *Widro*

"A man without imagination is like a bird without wings."
-*Wilhelm Raabe*

"Cowards die many times before their deaths, the valiant never taste of death but once."
- *Shakespeare*

We erect many individual barriers which also rob us of our creativity. Avoiding the design of a logo due to our lack of formal training in commercial art may be a result of fear. Fear of failure is one of the more effective robbers of our creativity. Along with fear stand laziness and perception. Both of these can interfere with our willingness to accept the challenge of designing a company logo or undertaking new projects in our lives.

Laziness is due to a lack of self motivation. Motivational experts state that only 10% of the North American population is self or internallly motivated. If we only allow ourselves to be externally motivated, we will not likely undertake the tasks needed to discover and recognize our creative abilities.

We generate many perceptions in our lifes which are not necessarily representative of reality. The perception that we cannot design a good logo because we have no formal training is a good example. This perception is false since most of us who are not artistic are so because we have not made the effort to be artistic. Once we make the effort, we all can design a logo.

Perception can distort many of life's realities. Let's look at the following exercises to see how easily our perception can interfere with the true picture.

Exercise #2-2 - Looking At Perception

Take a glance at the following three figures and write down what you saw on a separate piece of paper.

Figure #2-1

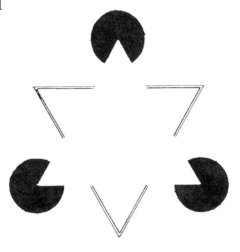

Figure #2-2

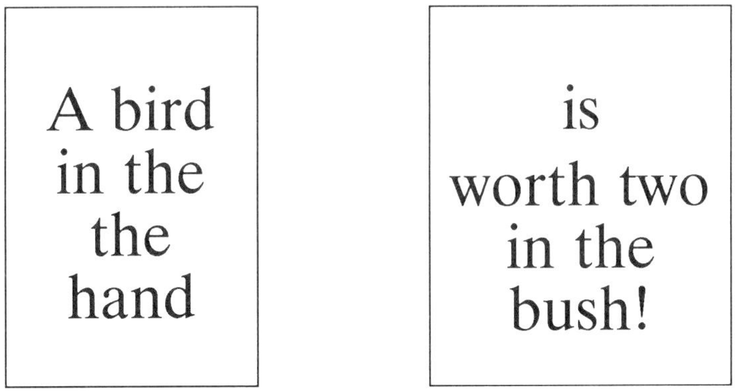

| A bird in the the hand | is worth two in the bush! |

Figure #3

The above figures can offer some proof that we do not always perceive things as well as we think we do.

In figure #1, you probably saw a triangle which is whiter than the rest of the page. Note first that there is no actual triangle drawn there. Your eyes just imagined one being there based on the other figures. In addition the whiteness of this mirage triangle is no brighter than the rest of the page. Just as we see a triangle and brightness that is not in this figure, we tend to perceive many things in life that are not there. These can take the form of imagined barriers to creativity that are not really there.

If you saw everything there was to see in figure #2, you should have read the following in the two boxes.

A bird in the the hand is worth two in the bush.

Not seeing the two the's is a case of not seeing what is actually there. In life we tend to do the same thing. We may see only one solution and not the many solutions that exist to our problems.

Figure #3 is a photo of an advertisement for a woman's consumer trade show. This is an interesting example of what we can see if we take the time to look. Note there is a silhouette of a man's face in the woman's hair right under "Be all that you can be." Over 95% of the people will not see this with their first look. Was this silhouette intentional on the artist's part? What do you think?

EXERCISES

BARRIERS TO CREATIVITY

Attempt the following exercises as a test of your creative abilities. You may have seen these exercises before. If you know a solution, then think up of others. Remember that creativity is going beyond what you already know to something new. Knowledge of the old is not creativity.

Exercise #2-3 - The "Old Nine Into Six" Trick

Make the Roman Numeral nine into a six by adding just one line.

I X

Exercise #2-4 (a) - The "Classic Nine Circle" Exercise

Connect all the nine circles below using FOUR straight lines without lifting your pen or pencil from the surface.

O   O   O

O   O   O

O   O   O

Exercise #2-4 (b)

Now connect all the nine circles with THREE straight lines without taking your pen or pencil off the surface.

Exercise #2-4 (c)

Now connect all the nine circles with JUST ONE straight line without taking your pen or pencil off the surface.

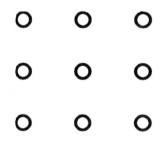

Chapter 2 Notes

Exercise #2-3

The standard solution to this exercise is the following one which is arrived at by overcoming the barriers of thinking of a line as a straight line only and of being restricted to making a Roman numeral six.

S I X

Note: Knowing the above solution from having read about it or having been shown it before is not a sign of creativity. This is just knowledge. Creativity is finding a new solution which you did not know about. **There are at least four other solutions to this exercise.** See if you can get any of them. Another solution is given on the following page.

Exercise #2-4 (a)

The following solution is the one normally used. **Note again** that this exercise has many solutions. A seminar presenter in the USA professes to have accumulated **25 different solutions** over the years. See how many others you can get.

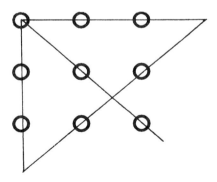

Exercise #2-4 (b)

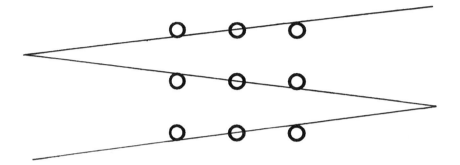

Exercise #2-4 (c)

Some people claim this one is impossible. Yet I have <u>6 different</u> <u>solutions</u> for doing this with one straight line without taking the pen or pencil off the surface. Here is one of them. (This can be accomplished by cutting the paper and putting all the nine circles in a row before drawing the line.)

Exercise #2-3 (continued)

Add this solid line and turn the paper upside down to get VI.

CHAPTER 3

Do Be Do Be Do

"My life is filled with many
obstacles. The greatest
obstacle is me."

- Jack Parr

"To be is to do."

- Camus

"To do is to be."

- Sartre

"Do be do be do."

- Frank Sinatra

LIGHTING THE FLAME RATHER THAN BEING WARMED BY IT

I don't like drinking either! But I am an entrepreneur and booze helps me be more creative.

Exercise #3-1 - Having What It Takes To Be Creative

Which of the following factors is essential for us to be creative?

_____ a) Being born creative

_____ b) Having had the right parents

_____ c) Having the right education

_____ d) Being right brained rather than left brained

_____ e) Having a high IQ

Creativity is thought to be a matter of special skill, ability, knowledge or effort. In fact, it is not! Anyone can be creative. None of the above factors is an essential foundation for creative success. If you take a hard look at creative people, they are simply "being" creative. They are coming from excellence and creativity because they made the choice. There is no expectation of having some factor beyond their control make them creative. They realize they have to light the flame rather than be warmed by it.

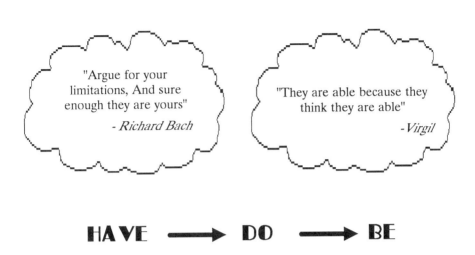

"Argue for your limitations, And sure enough they are yours"
- *Richard Bach*

"They are able because they think they are able"
-*Virgil*

HAVE ➔ DO ➔ BE

There are those who believe that the above sequence represents the road to creativity. Their belief is that a person must first "HAVE" what creative people have; inherited intelligence, high education, a good job, money and a host of other things. Then the person will "DO" what creative people do. Finally the person will "BE" creative. This belief is false. There is no truth to the belief that creative people have special things that enable them to be creative and non-creative people do not have these things. The fact of the matter is non-creative people have all the things necessary to be creative.

Reversing the above sequence better represents the road to creativity. The right order is from "BEING" to "DOING" to "HAVING".

BE ➔ DO ➔ HAVE

First we must choose to "BE" creative. Then we will "DO" the things creative people do. What will follow naturally is we will "HAVE" the things that creative people have. The "HAVE" things include the ability to cope with and enjoy a rapidly changing world. There are also the sense of accomplishment, satisfaction and happiness generated from attempting and completing challenging activities.

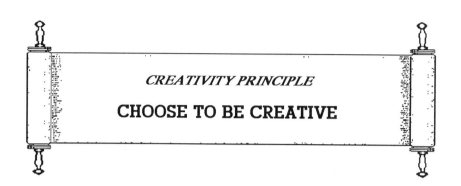

CREATIVITY PRINCIPLE

CHOOSE TO BE CREATIVE

The major difference between creative people and non-creative people is two fold. First creative people believe that they can be creative. They know that creativity can be learned. Creative people do not deny their abilities and potentials. Second creative people know they have to get themselves moving. They realize that they have to choose to be creative.

People Choosing To Be Creative

☆ Until recently, Ted Endicott was the top retail car salesperson for General Motors anywhere. In one 11 month period he had sold 456 cars. His monthly sales averaged about 40 cars a month. Not too bad considering that the national average is about 10 cars a month. Endicott's 1987 earnings were $125,000. The one thing you should know about Endicott is that he became blind after selling cars for 27 years. Did he quit? No he didn't. He chose to adjust to his handicap. His impressive sales continued due to his creativity in dealing with his handicap. Most customers didn't realize he was blind until after the sale.

☆ Dave Schwartz is the founder and chairman of the board of Rent-A-Wreck®, the world's largest used-car rental agency. Like many entrepreneurs, Dave faced what seemed like an insurmountable problem. He could not get capital financing to expand his business. Not having a high education or the business contacts did not stop Schwartz. He figured out how to expand without any capital.

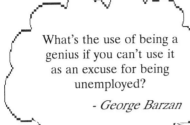

> What's the use of being a
> genius if you can't use it
> as an excuse for being
> unemployed?
>
> *- George Barzan*

> There is nothing so
> irritating as somebody
> with less intelligence and
> more sense than we have.
>
> *- Don Herold*

TOO INTELLECTUAL TO BE CREATIVE?

Seymour Epstein, a psychologist at the University of Massachusetts, has found that constructive thinking is crucial for life success. Constructive thinking has almost nothing to do with our IQ. Constructive thinking involves taking action about a situation rather than complaining about it. It also involves the ability to not take things personally and not fret about what others think of us. Constructive thinking determines a great range of life's successes, from salaries and promotions, to happiness with friendships, to physical and emotional health.

Epstein found that many academically bright people do not think constructively. They have self-destructive habits of mind. They hold back from new challenges because they lack the necessary emotional smarts. Emotional intelligence was found by Epstein to be more important than academic intelligence.

Epstein's findings should not surprise many of us. We are already aware that many people with PhD's are not very creative and some of the most creative people around don't even know what a PhD is.

Why don't more people choose to be constructive thinkers? My personal theory is that it is because becoming a constructive thinker takes effort and change. Most people resist anything that requires effort or change. Given the choice of doing something that is easy or something that is difficult, most people will opt for the easy. Why? Short term comfort appeals to people.

The choice of comfort is a paradox. Choosing to avoid the difficult is more comfortable in the short term; however, in the long term it results in discomfort. Most of us need to have tackled and conquered challenging tasks before we experience a sense of accomplishment and satisfaction.

~~PAYING~~ ENJOYING THE PRICE

Figure #3-1 represents what I call the "Easy Rule Of Life". Note this is the way life is. Please don't blame me for the way it is. I didn't set it up this way. I just observed that life is this way and we have to make the best of it. The real prizes in life come to us when we are willing to do things somewhat difficult and uncomfortable. Choosing to be creative is one of them.

There is a price to pay in making the effort to be creative, just as there is in anything worthwhile in life. But rather than looking at the prices we have to pay, let us look at the many "prices we get to enjoy". Prices to enjoy include: higher self-esteem, greater satisfaction, increased happiness, and more peace of mind. Indeed the price is to be more enjoyed than paid.

Figure #3-1 - The Easy Rule Of Life

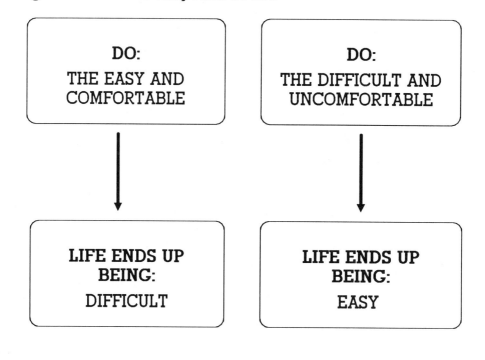

CHAPTER 4

101 Ways To Skin A Cat Or Do Business

"Say what you will about the Ten Commandments, you must always come back to the pleasant fact that there are only ten of them."

-H. L. Mencken

"He was distinguished for ignorance; for he had only one idea, and that was wrong."

- Benjamin Disraeli

GETTING THE "RIGHT ANSWER"

I have been watching this game show for 7 years and I
have never been able to answer even one question.

Let us begin this chapter with the following two exercises.

Exercise #4-1

Matthew Reich was about to introduce his "New Amsterdam Beer" to the extremely competitive market in New York. He had a major problem: no money to advertise his product. Reich was able to generate substantial sales in a relatively short period despite this major problem. His creative approach led to 1987 sales of $4.5 million.

How would you have handled the problem of no money for advertising to launch a new beer in a competitive market?

Exercise #4-2 - The Unique Pair Of Scissors

Which pair of scissors is different from all of the others?

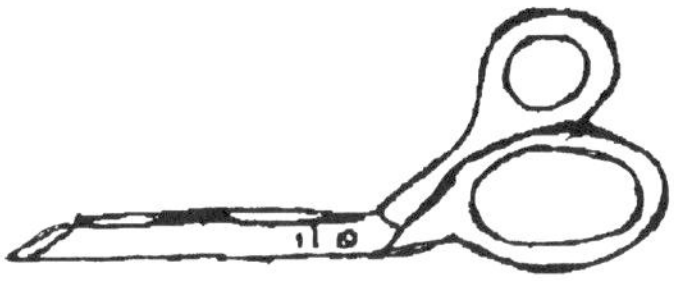

A

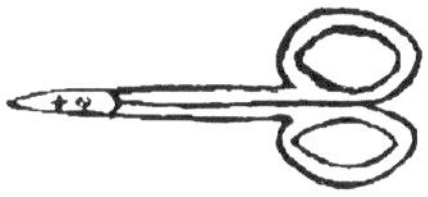

B

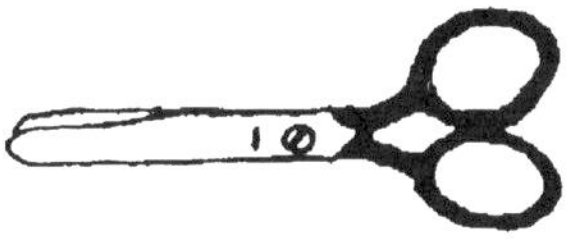

C

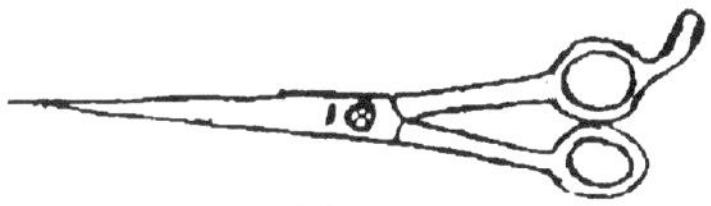

D

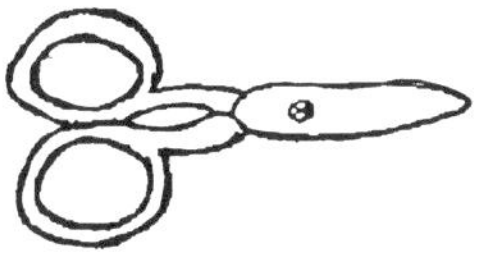

E

101 WAYS TO SKIN A CAT, DO BUSINESS OR ...

A North American and a European were discussing the joys of life when the European stated that he knew 100 different ways to make love. The North American was highly impressed with this. He told the European he knew only one. The European asked him which one it was. The North American described the most natural and conventional way there is. The European then replied to the North American "That is amazing! I never thought of that! Thanks. Now I know 101."

Are you like the North American or the European when solving problems? Do you come up with only one solution or many? We have all heard the saying "there is more than one way to skin a cat." Yet how many of us would look for several ways to skin a cat if we had to skin one.

Most of us are apt to look for one way to do most tasks. If this single way does not work well, we still stick with it and find someone or something to blame for the situation being unworkable. We do not look for new ways. Another way may be quicker, more efficient, or less costly. Last but not least, it could plainly be more fun. Ask the European if you ever run into him.

Let us return to exercise #4-1. Were you looking for the one right way of overcoming the problem? Did you stop after one solution or did you come up with many alternatives? How Matthew Reich handled it is not the only way (see chapter notes). Many solutions are available. Reich could have borrowed money for advertising. He could have sold shares in his company to generate additional money for advertising. Partnership with an established brewery was an option as was generating publicity through some off-beat activity. The list of options is endless.

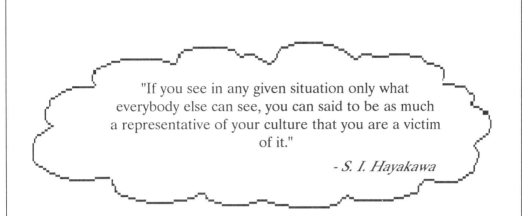

"If you see in any given situation only what everybody else can see, you can said to be as much a representative of your culture that you are a victim of it."

- S. I. Hayakawa

Exercise #4-2 gives more evidence of how we approach problems. Did you overlook the obvious like nine out of ten people do on this exercise. Ninety percent of participants in my seminars and classes end up choosing one of the five pairs of scissors. Everyone is right to a certain degree but most participants miss the main point. That is because the answer is *"all the pairs of scissors are different from all the others".*

This exercise demonstrates how well the school systems have taught us to automatically look for the one right answer or one way of doing things. In doing so we become very structured in our responses. We tend to stop looking for more "right answers". Then when the only "right" answer we came up with is a "dud", we are lost.

One of the most important creativity principles is there are two or more solutions to all problems. Two exceptions to the rule exist. One is in mathematics. Half of 13 has only one answer. (Note we will see in Chapter 9 that even this problem may have more than one solution.) In mathematics most problems have one solution. The only other time there are less than two solutions is when we are dead. Then there are no solutions. Generally speaking life's problems have two or more solutions.

Possibility in life's situations extends beyond the available and obvious. What do we have to do to create many new solutions? It is essential we first let go of the old and go to a state of nothing. Yes we must start from nothing. Opportunity is literally created from a state of nothingness. When we let go of old solutions and old ways of thinking, we have a clear slate to create from. Human rights, Einstein's theory of relativity, and Gandhi's India were literallly created from nothing. So were many business ventures such as the pet rock and the hoola hoop.

Looking for options requires effort. It is easier to look for alternatives when we are dissatisfied with the alternatives we have at hand. However we should look for more solutions even when the ones we already have appeal to us. Care should be taken in not necessarily limiting ourselves to the first few alternatives we generate. Disciplining ourselves to keep looking for other alternatives, even when we are satisfied with some of those already generated, is a good practice.

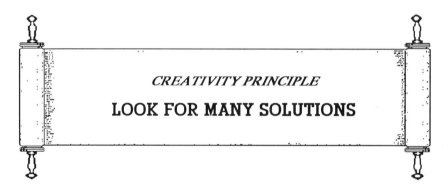

CREATIVITY PRINCIPLE

LOOK FOR **MANY SOLUTIONS**

The point is that better solutions and alternatives should be strived for even when things appear to be going well. Attempts at inventing better alternatives when a good one is already available has three main benefits:

- ✓ This provides some insurance that a better alternative has not been overlooked. The successful alternative in use may not be the best available.

- ✓ Most, if not all, good things come to an end. People, who generate alternatives when things are going well, have other solutions to fall back on when the present solution is no longer effective due to changing circumstances.

- ✓ People continually involved in the selection of alternatives, whether needed or not, will keep their creative talents in practice for when they are needed.

The old adage "If it works, don't fix it" is questionable in this day and age. Even is it is working fine, it probably won't for very long in a competitive and rapidly changing business world. Having the ability to generate many solutions allows us to react much more effectively when it does break down.

Exercise #4-3   A QUOTA OF NEW IDEAS

Do this exercise regularly. Set a goal to generate at least 3 new ideas daily for your most important project or problem.

Exercise #4-4   PLAYING WITH MATCHES

In preparation for the next chapter, let us try another type of exercise. Assume the following two equations are made with matchsticks. Each line in the characters is one matchstick. Both equations are wrong as they stand. Can you by moving just one matchstick make the equation correct. Proceed to exercise (b) when you have completed (a).

(a)

$$VI + II = VI$$

(b)

$$VI - IV = IX$$

Chapter 4 Notes

Exercises

#4-1

Matthew Reich came up with a plan to place the beer in the trendiest restaurants where the beer would be consumed by the "right people". He figured if they liked his beer, they would tell business associates and social contacts. When Reich first approached many restaurants, he was shunned and laughed at.

He responded by using a principle of creativity. He became persistent. For example, he ate in one restaurant for three weeks and became friends with the bartender. The bartender agreed to feature his beer in that outlet. Eventually Reich generated enough interest so that his plan worked. In fact he believes that "I don't think we would have been as successful if we had advertised."

#4-2

They are all different from all the others.

#4-4

These two exercises are a test for how well you mastered the principle of looking for more than one solution. Notice how easy it is to stop after we have one solution. If you did not get at least 3 solutions to both exercises, you are in the majority. In my seminars, over 85% of the participants stop after one solution even though I have just emphasized the creativity principle of looking for more than one solution.

Exercise (a) has at least seven solutions and (b) has at least five. Now go back and try again.

CHAPTER 5

A Great Memory For Forgetting

"I always have trouble remembering three things: faces, names, and -- I can't remember what the third thing is"

-Fred Allen

"I finally got it all together and then I forgot where I put it."

- Anon

IS YOUR PHOTOGRAPHIC
MEMORY OUT OF FILM?

*"While golfing I had a stunning idea on how to save the
company from going under but I forgot it."*

How good is your memory? The intent of this chapter is to underscore the importance of writing our ideas down. We have a tendency to avoid writing down ideas thinking that we will remember them later. This is a mistake. We are not as good at remembering things as we think we are.

The following exercises will demonstrate this.

Exercise #5-1 - I'm Too Old To Remember That!

Draw the dial of a non-digital telephone, that is one with a finger dial rather than a touch-tone one. Place all the finger holes in their right position on the dial and then record the position of all the numbers and letters. This is something that you have seen many times so it will not be a problem to remember, right!

Now refer to the back of this chapter and see how you did on the above Exercise #5-1. If you didn't get the non-digital telephone dial completely, you are definitely in the majority. Most of us have a hard time remembering what the dial precisely looks like. Let us try another exercise.

Exercise #5-2 - Remembering A Robbery

Recall the cartoon with the two robbers in Chapter #2. Assume you witnessed that attempted robbery and have been asked by the police department to identify the two robbers. Without looking back at the cartoon on page 22, try to pick the two men out of the 12 in the following figure who were attempting the creativity robbery.

"I'm still chasing girls. I don't remember what for, but I'm still chasing them."

- Joe E. Lewis

"When you are right no one remembers, when you are wrong no one forgets."

- Red Smith

By now some of you are probably getting worried about your memories being shot because of your age. Not so. Look at children. Ask a school teacher whether children forget things at school. The school teacher will list things like coats, lunchpails, gloves, books, combs, pencils, pens, and much more. Children don't forget because of their age. Neither do we. We forget because of the many distractions we have in our lives.

Not remembering the dial on the telephone or the two faces in a picture is not a serious thing. However forgetting good ideas for our problems may cost us wonderful or blockbuster solutions. Ideas are easy to forget. Exercise #5-3 may give more evidence of this.

Exercise #5-3 - Thinking About Your Past Thinking

Write down the thoughts that you were thinking at exactly this time of the day one week ago. In addition write down all the good ideas you had about solutions to your problems, someone else's problems, or to society's problems in the last week.

How did you do? If you could not remember much about what you were thinking one week ago, how do you know if you have forgotten one or more blockbuster ideas that you had right at that time. How about all the ideas during the week since then. Possibly you had some useful ideas that you did not write down and have since forgotten.

To deal with the tendency of their employees forgetting good ideas, some organizations have installed locker rooms in their work premises. Writing pads and pens have been placed in these locker rooms. These are for recording ideas that the employees may think of while exercising or in the shower. There is a good reason for this practice. Many good ideas are generated when people exercise. Good ideas tend to come from the altered states of mind that exercise produces. The companies want to be sure that most of the ideas are recorded immediately and not lost with time.

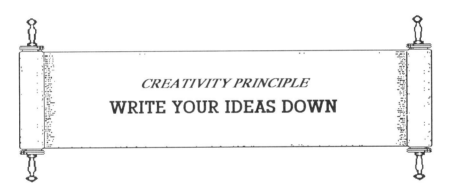

CREATIVITY PRINCIPLE

WRITE YOUR IDEAS DOWN

If our ideas are not recorded immediately, we risk not recalling them later. What causes this tendency to not recall ideas at a later time is our changed state of mind. Our minds are overworked trying to remember the many things for everyday living. When we become totally engrossed in something else related to other work assignments or to our personal lives, the last thing on our minds are the good ideas we had a day or two ago while in the shower.

To totally convince yourself about the importance of recording your ideas and solutions, do one last exercise over a period of time. When you are working on a special project, write down all the ideas that you get and put them in a file. Be extremely disciplined about this. Don't forget to record anything. Do this for two weeks and during these two weeks do not review the contents of the file. At the end of the two weeks try and remember everything that went in the file. Then look in the file. You may be surprised at the number of ideas that you have forgotten.

IDEA TREES

Writing your ideas, answers, and solutions for a special problem or project can be done in many different forms. You can either make a list, use sentences, or write an essay. These all have their places; however, there is a better tool for recording ideas. This device is especially useful in the initial stages of solving the problem or working on a project.

The tool is an idea tree. Other names by which this tool is also known include mind map, spoke diagram, thought web, and clustering diagram. The idea tree is simple but powerful. The surprising thing is that most of us were never shown how to use an idea tree when attending our educational system. I first learned about it from a waiter in a restaurant.

Here is how an idea tree is created. Starting at the center of the page, the goal, theme, or purpose of the tree is recorded. For example if you are generating an idea tree for the ways in which you want to market a new management book, you can write this down as in Figure 5-1.

From the central theme, branches or lines are drawn towards the boundary of the page. On these branches are printed any ideas that relate to the problem or project. Primary ideas are recorded on separate branches near the center of the page. Secondary branches are then drawn exiting from the primary ones. This is where the secondary ideas that relate to the main ones are recorded. More branches off the secondary ones can be drawn which will record a third level of ideas.

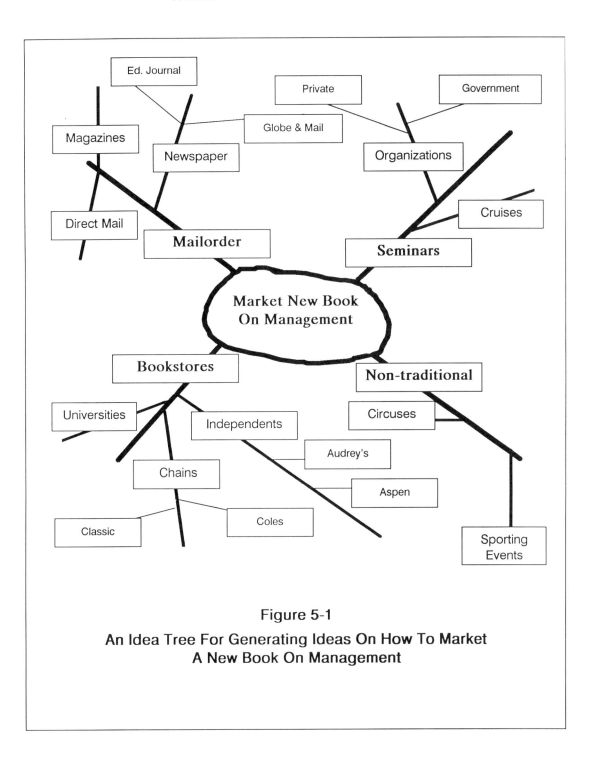

Figure 5-1

An Idea Tree For Generating Ideas On How To Market
A New Book On Management

One primary idea for marketing a new management book is to market the book in bookstores. The word "Bookstores" is recorded as one of the primary ideas on the idea tree in Figure 5-1. Then secondary ideas are generated to enlarge on the types of bookstores. Chains, university, and independent bookstores are listed on the second level of ideas. A third level of ideas is used to enlarge on the chain bookstores. Here we include the Coles and the Classic chains. More levels of ideas can be added if needed.

This tool is a powerful way of generating a lot of ideas quickly. Although the idea tree is meant to be a tool for individual brainstorming, it can be adapted for group use without any problems. Let us look at the reasons for the effectiveness of the idea tree as an idea-generating tool.

Advantages Of The Idea Tree

- ✓ It is compact. Many ideas can be listed on one page. If needed, the idea tree can be expanded to additional pages.
- ✓ Ideas are put in categories. This makes it easier to group ideas.
- ✓ The creator of an idea tree can hitchhike on his or her own ideas to generate many other ideas. This works in much the same way as hitchhiking in group brainstorming.
- ✓ It is a long-term tool. After setting it aside for a day or a week, the person using the tree can come back and generate a batch of fresh ideas.

Idea trees are not only used for the right-brain activity of rapid-idea generation. Another way to use an idea tree is for the purpose of self-discovery by way of clustering thoughts about such things as what is your relationship with money.

Left-brain activities such as planning and organizing also lend themselves to being performed on idea trees. Short-range plans, long-range plans, diaries, speech plans, goals, and records of lecture notes can be done with this useful tool.

Who of major consequence has used idea trees? Only such people as Albert Einstein, Leonardo Da Vinci, Thomas Jefferson, John F. Kennedy, and Thomas Edison. I think this is a good group with which to be associated.

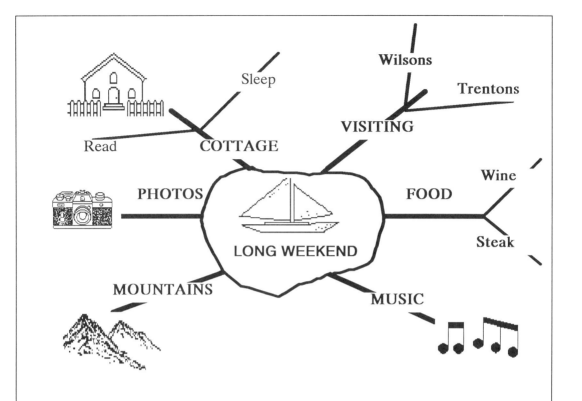

Figure 5-2

**An Idea Tree (Using Visuals) For Generating Ideas On
What To Do On A Long Weekend**

Figure 5-2 shows a more advanced idea tree which uses images. Images are used to enhance creativity and memory. Colour can be used along with images to add to the effects of the idea tree.

Idea trees require more work than do ordinary lists; however, the extra work is well worth it. Remember "the easy rule of life" from page 38 in chapter 3. By putting in the extra work in constructing this more difficult and challenging tool, you will be a lot better off in the long run than you are with ordinary lists or by not using any tool at all.

<u>Chapter 5 Notes</u>

Exercises

#5-1

Not one in a thousand people in my seminars will get this exactly. Note that there are somethings you did not notice about the telephone dial even though you have seen it many times. These are things that were staring you in the face but you never saw. Why? You never put in the effort to look. Similarly many solutions to our problems stare us in our faces. We do not see these solutions because of our lack of effort in looking.

a) The 1 has no letters beside it.

b) The Q and Z are not used.

c) The letters go clockwise in ABC, DEF, GHI and JKL. The letters go counterclockwise in all the other sets of three letters.

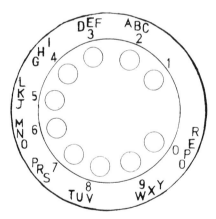

#5-2

B and L

CHAPTER 6

The Advantages Of Drinking On The Job

"Good judgment comes from experience; and experience, well, that comes from bad judgment."

- Anon

"I drink to make my friends seem interesting."

-Anon

My Design For A New Tandem Bicycle

The best way to emphasize the point of this chapter is for us to start with the following exercise.

Exercise #6-1

You have been hired by a major bicycle manufacturer as a consultant. Your job is to evaluate the merits of the bicycle designs that designers submit to the manufacturer. The manufacturer has asked for a new design for a tandem bicycle.

One of the designs that the manufacturer received is the one above. This is one that I as a novice designer am proposing. (It was the best one I could come up with.)

Write down the main points about the design of my tandem bicycle that you will put in your report to the manufacturer. Be honest in your evaluation and do not be afraid of hurting my ego.

Let's look at my bicycle design in Exercise #6-1. What points did you choose for your report? Are your points all negative? If they are, you have not explored my design fully. Unless you put down some positive points, some negative points, and some in between, you have jumped to conclusions without due consideration to my "wonderful" design for a new bicycle. Your voice of judgment (VOJ) has stepped in too soon.

You should have considered such positive points as the rear wheel can be used as a spare for the front in case the front tire goes flat. How about a more comfortable ride because of two back wheels. This bicycle could also have an advantage over conventional ones for carrying heavy loads. It is great for overweight people. People may want to buy it as a status symbol since it is a new and different design.

On the negative side, the bicycle may be awkward to ride. The back wheel may be excess baggage. It looks ridiculous. There is no second seat for an extra person.

There are many points to be made for both the positve and negative aspects of this design. To fully explore the merits of this design, we should write down and consider all these points. Then we can make a decision based on a comprehensive evaluation of this new idea for a bicycle.

Exercise #6-2

SUGGESTION:
Our new promotional flyers belong in washroom stalls.

You are the owner of a medium size advertising agency. To remain competitive, your company is looking for new markets and new opportunities. Two weeks ago you introduced a suggestion box to encourage new ideas from the employees. As you are going through the latest ideas in the suggestion box, a rather odd suggestion appears. The suggestion says "Our new promotional flyers belong in washroom stalls."

What should you do with this suggestion?

1. Assume it is a practical joke, chuckle and disregard it.

2. Assume it means that the new flyers are ineffective.

3. Assume the idea is serious but the person who made it is demented.

4. Assume the idea is serious and has some merits for consideration.

"When a true genius appears in the world, you will know him by this sign, that all the dunces are in confederacy against him."

- Jonathan Swift

"A man with a new idea is a crank until the idea succeeds."

- Mark Twain

VOJ - THE IDEA DESTROYER

Your voice of judgment (VOJ) may have affected the answer that you chose in Exercise #6-2? Did you choose to ignore or eliminate the washroom stalls as a viable advertising medium? If you did, think again. An entrepreneur in the USA is generating millions of dollars of revenue annually by selling advertising space in washrooms of businesses and airplanes. The idea was spawned when he left sales brochures in washrooms and he started getting great responses. One of the biggest advantages is that the audience is more captive with this form of advertising than many others. If you did not give this advertising medium any consideration, it is because you were the victim of your voice of judgment. This prevented you from fully exploring this idea for its full potential.

We are all victims of our voices of judgment. This is the rational part of us that can jump in and destroy an idea before it has a chance to blossom. Many good ideas are not given full consideration. We tend to find something negative about these ideas and promptly discard them. The reverse is also true. We may promptly accept an idea without looking at all the negatives.

Suggestion boxes offer some evidence of the power of people's VOJ. Some companies report that over 50% of their employees' ideas have merit. Other companies report that less than 5% of employees' suggestions have any value. Why the big difference? Surely more than 5% of ideas in any company are useful. In all likelihood, the mangement of companies which use only a minute number of all ideas submitted are discarding a lot of good ideas. They do not fully explore them for all the positives. They focus on the negatives and discard ideas without any further consideration.

"GREAT WACKY" IDEAS SAVED FROM THE VOJ

Many successful ideas have been spared death by others' VOJ because the originators of these ideas had the presence of mind to fully explore them for their value. The majority of people in our society would not have given these ideas any consideration whatsoever. Yet due to the ideas' success, they are taken for granted as being the norm for today.

☆ By accidently preparing grain too long in the oven, the Kellogg brothers in the late 1800's wound up with what today is known as cornflakes. They decided to introduce this product as a cold cereal. Up until that time cereal was always eaten hot. When first introduced, nearly all the industry marketing experts predicted imminent failure for the product. They labelled it "Horsefood".

> **ABSOLUTELY**
> **NEW!**
>
> **SPECIAL K**
> **HORSEFOOD**

☆ Over ten years ago, Bill Comrie along with two partners took over his father's small furniture sales store in Edmonton, Alberta. Today Bill Comrie owns the Brick Furniture stores which comprise one of the biggest furniture chains in North America. One of Comrie's first marketing tools was the "Midnight Madness Sale." The first one he proposed was questioned by his two partners. They claimed no one would show up. Well show up they did. The furniture store did more business during that one night than Bill Comrie's father had done in the previous year in the store. The "Midnight Madness Sale" was used with great success in the early days of The Brick's phenomenal growth.

☆ On the night that the idea for the Pet Rock was conceived, several people laughed and joked about this great pet that everyone would want. Of course this was a ridiculous idea to everyone except for Gary Dahl. He went home and could not sleep because of the idea's promise. It was then that he overcame his VOJ and decided to market a book giving instructions on how to care for a Pet Rock. Its success is history.

"POST-IT NOTES" ® - SAVED FROM THE VOJ

The idea of Post-It Notes originated in 1974 with Art Fry, a 3M employee who sang in a choir. He used bits of paper to mark the hymns but the papers kept falling out of his books. He went into the office one day and made some papers with adhesive backing. These worked well. When 3M decided to look into marketing a commerical variation of these notes, distributors thought they were silly. Initial market surveys offered little promise. The 3M company did not allow others' voices of judgment to interfere with the development of this product. A mailing of samples to secretaries of large companies showed a favourable interest. Introduced in 1980, the notes now bring in over $200 million dollars in annual revenue to the 3M corporation.

A GOOD IDEA - DON'T BANK ON IT

You are not the only individual who has had problems with bankers. A banker once told Alexander Graham Bell to get out of his bank with "that ridiculous toy". This so called ridiculous toy was one of Bell's first innovative models of the telephone.

Getting your banker to think positively about your product may be quite a challenge. In one of my seminar presentations to a banking institution, I used Exercise #6-1 to determine whether its bank managers fully explore ideas; that is evaluate ideas on both positive and negative qualities. Out of about 10 comments, there was not one positive one. Considering that the bicycle does has some good attributes, I had to conclude that these bankers were trained to, above all, focus on the negatives. It is no wonder that many good business proposals will receive little financial support from most banks.

PMI - THE IDEA SAVIOUR

The PMI method is a powerful thinking tool developed by Edward de Bono. It is powerful but yet so simple. Everybody will think they use it all the time; however, a lot of people do not use it at all. In fact, highly intellectual people are more prone that others to not utilize this method because of their confidence in their viewpoint as being the only right one.

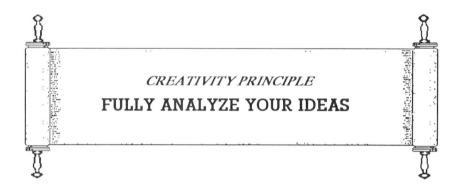

CREATIVITY PRINCIPLE

FULLY ANALYZE YOUR IDEAS

The PMI method of thinking is a tool used over a period of a few minutes (two to five) to focus attention on the idea on hand. It is deliberate and is performed in a very disciplined manner to give a more complete exploration of the idea.

PMI is an abbreviation for the types of things that one should consider in the analysis of an idea or a solution to a problem. The letters stand for the following:

☞ P stands for Plus (positive points)

☞ M stands for Minus (negative points)

☞ I stands for Interesting (neutral points)

Example - PMI As An Idea Analyzer

If we were to ask 50 people what they thought about the idea of the government giving everyone $5000 to stimulate the economy, a majority may think it is a good idea. Then if we asked these same persons to reconsider using the PMI method of thinking, we would undoubtedly get some different results. The PMI analysis could look something like this:

PLUS	MINUS	INTERESTING
⇨ more spending will result	⇨ our taxes will go up	⇨ interesting to see how much money is banked
⇨ people will be happier	⇨ drug addicts will buy drugs and alcoholics will drink themselves silly	⇨ interesting to see what people will spend money on
⇨ more jobs will be created	⇨ more resources will be used up	⇨ interesting to see if charitable donations increase
⇨ children will leave home	⇨ inflation increase	
	⇨ children will leave home	

Note the "INTERESTING" component of the PMI technique has several uses. First, the comments which are neither favorable nor unfavorable can be placed here. Second, the thinker is encouraged to look outside the normal judgmental framework of good or bad. Last, this aspect can lead the thinker to look at another idea by hitchhiking on the one being considered.

When people force themselves to use the PMI method, they usually find that their feelings about the topic change from what they felt at the outset. The final decision can be somewhat of a surprise to themselves. PMI is most useful in those situations where we feel sure about our conclusion from the outset. That is when we need to use this form of analysis the most.

Exercise #6-3 - Ideas To PMI

Allowing three minutes for each one, analyze the following ideas:

A. Everyone should be paid the same salary no matter what their occupation.
B. We should all be fired after five years at any job.
C. We should allow employees to drink alcoholic beverages at work.

PLUS	MINUS	INTERESTING

Notes To Yourself

CHAPTER 7

Goaling For It!

"It's just as difficult to reach
a destination you don't
have, as it is to come back
from a place you've never
been."

-Zig Ziglar

"By the time we've made it,
we've had it."

- Malcolm Forbes

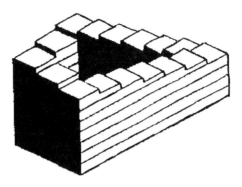

THE ILLUSION OF ACTIVITY AND WANTS

If you were to walk in a clockwise direction on the walls of the above figure, you would think you were going up. It would appear to you that you were destined for greater heights. However in no time you would realize that you are back at the same level that you started. No matter how much energy you put into walking up the steps, higher levels would just be illusions.

Such is the illusion of activity without well-defined goals. Many people misconstrue their unplanned activity as a direction in life. They wind up putting a lot of energy into these non-goals and end up getting nowhere. Activity is necessary in reaching greater heights, but greater heights only come with defined goals. If we are to arrive at new and worthwhile destinations, we must begin by first defining these destinations. The journey has direction once the destination is set.

The most important point in defining goals is knowing where we want to go or what we want to accomplish. If there is anything that will keep us from gettting what we want in life, it is not knowing what we want. Our parents want us to want certain things. Our friends want us to want. Society wants us to want. Advertisers want us to want. These are our non-wants; the question is what do we truly want for ourselves.

Why is it that many of us do not know what we want? We haven't really put much effort into finding out. Where do we want to journey? We can find this out only by taking the time to truly know ourselves. Once we get in touch with our essence we will know what we want and where we want to go without needing someone else to tell us what is important to us.

ISN'T GOAL SETTING UNCREATIVE?

Is the setting of goals a structuring of activity? Doesn't creativity require unstructured activity? The answer to both of these questions is yes. Remember that creative success is the result of both soft and hard thinking. These two types of thinking respectively translate into unstructured and structured mental activities. By setting goals, we are adding some of the needed structure to our mission of being creative.

Planning is important to innovation. Don't most plans fail? Yes they do. Someone once remarked that "all plans fail and planning is invaluable". Most plans do not work out exactly the way we want them to. This means a lot of our goals will not be realized in the exact form we define nor within the time frame we set. Nonetheless goal setting is extremely valuable.

Goals give us something to strive for that we would not otherwise strive for. They give us a purpose. Once we have a purpose and a direction, we have reasons for being innovative and creative. It makes little sense to generate a lot of solutions without a purpose. People tend to be much more creative when they have something to work towards.

Many individuals and organizations become highly creative when a big problem or a disaster arises. They respond in creative ways because there is a need to do so. After Apple Computers became successful with their personal computer, IBM had no choice but to invent one themselves if they wanted to tap some of this lucrative market. The goal was clear: Come up with a new personal computer in a short time frame. IBM responded by setting up a group of managers and designers who worked independently of IBM's central bureaucracy. This allowed the group to work in an environment which was conducive to innovation. The well-defined goal was what was needed to motivate IBM's managers and designers to be creative. The result was the highly-successful IBM personal computer.

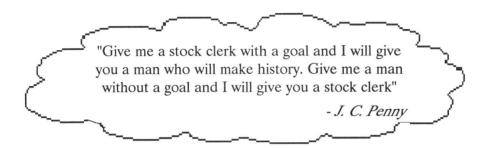

"Give me a stock clerk with a goal and I will give you a man who will make history. Give me a man without a goal and I will give you a stock clerk"

- J. C. Penny

WHY MOST PEOPLE DON'T "GOAL FOR IT"

Researchers say that only about 10% of the population in North America have well-defined goals. This may appear surprisingly low for two countries which are known for their high achievers. Nonetheless, ten percent of millions of people still translates into a large number of goal seekers. These individuals constitute the minority who are doers. They have direction and make things happen. They set many goals and attain most of them.

So how about the rest fo the population? What stops the majority from investing the time to define their goals and work towards achieving them? Here are some of the reasons most people do not have goals.

* People are not convinced about the power of goal setting.

* Many people do not know what they want in life.

* Some people do not know how to set goals.

* Embarrassment is a worry for people who are afraid of not reaching their goals.

* Some people have such a low self image that they do not think they deserve to attain their goals.

There is one more reason. Goal setting takes effort and discipline. Once goals have been established, more effort and discipline are required in working towards the goals. Then even more effort and discipline are required to monitor the goals and set new ones. With all the effort and discipline required, many people decide against setting goals and working towards them.

Exercise #7-1 - Typical Goals That Don't Work

These are goals that people have set for themselves. Which of these are well-defined goals.

*   a) To have more money

*   b) To quit smoking

*   c) To write a book

*   d) To be a training specialist

*   e) To read more books over the next year

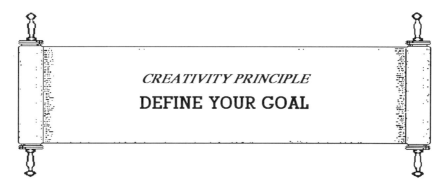

CREATIVITY PRINCIPLE

DEFINE YOUR GOAL

All of the above goals can be improved upon. Well-defined goals should abide by the following principles:

✓   Goals should have committment from the source (should be written down).

✓   Goals should be clearly defined and specific.

✓   Goals should be realistic, achievable, and measureable.

✓   Goals should have a target date and a cost limitation.

Last goals need an action plan to get us going. This tells us what we are going to do to get to where we are going. The action plan defines the type of activity we need to follow in our pursuit of our goals.

"All the way to heaven is heaven."

- St. Catherine of Siena

"The road is better than the inn."

- Cervantes

THE ULTIMATE GOAL IS THE PROCESS

The above ancient sayings bear out the importance of our being deeply involved in the process of attaining our goals. The process is more important than the actual goal attainment. Creative people extract more enjoyment and satisfaction from their efforts than from actually reaching their goals. The satisfaction from having reached a goal, no matter how significant, is usually short lived. Many people whose major goal is to be rich are in for a big surprise. A group of New York lottery winners experienced the opposite of what most people expect from a big win. This group formed the Millionaire Circle to deal with what they called "Post-Lottery Depression Syndrome".

Self-made millionaires tell us that goals as endpoints matter less than the process itself. Most successful entrepreneurs state that getting there was most of the fun. Some business people achieve their goal of financial independence and decide to take it easy. Most last two or three months before they get bored. They then develop new goals to pursue. Entrepreneurs seldom run out of goals because of their constant need for process.

Retired people offer more evidence. Many people who finally reach their goal of retirement find that their lives are worse than before. In fact, some retired people do not live very long after leaving the job. They become disenchanted because of their sudden loss of purpose. This absence of purpose is the result of not having more goals to pursue. Successfully retired people are not actually "retired". Retirement is another challenging process.

Robert Louis Stevenson said "To travel hopefully is a better thing than to arrive." Creative people know this. When the ultimate goal becomes the process, life changes. Creativity flows more readily. Failure is viewed as success. Losing means winning. The journey becomes the destination.

CHAPTER 8

In The Land
Of The Blind,
One Eye Is
King

"The obscure we see
eventuallly. The completely
obvious, it seems, takes
longer."

- Edward R. Murrow

"Common sense is not very
common."

-Latin Proverb

NOT SEEING WHAT IS THERE

It is always interesting to hear what participants in my seminars and courses see in the above figure. There have been a large number of different sightings. Some participants do not see anything. What do you see in it?

A consultant to restaurants in Western Canada makes a good living by saving restaurant operations from having to declare bankruptcy. What does he do that the owners are not able to do? Not much except that he is able to see the obvious. The consultant spots inefficiencies such as too many entrees on the menu. He may also see staff and equipment tied up in unproductive activities. Changes are made that could be recommended by just about anyone except by those directly associated with the restaurant. Many of these restaurants are saved because the obvious problems are pointed out to the owners. Without the consultant, they would not see the obvious and the restaurants would go into receivership.

Many times the best solutions are right before our eyes and we do not see them. The obvious escapes us. As the saying goes "We can't see the forest because of the trees". A character in Joseph Heller's "Catch 22" had flies in his eyes. He could not see these flies in his eyes. Reason: the flies in his eyes prevented him from seeing these same flies in his eyes. Often we are like this character in "Catch 22".

Incidentally, there is a Volkswagon Beetle in the previous figure. About one out of ten people spot this. Once you know it is there, try and not see it. Many things in life are this way. We won't see the obvious. However, once it is pointed out to us, we cannot help but see it.

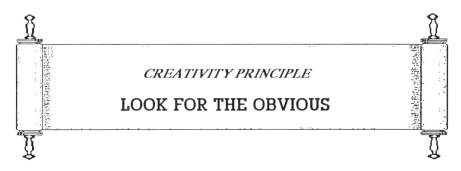

CREATIVITY PRINCIPLE

LOOK FOR THE OBVIOUS

The following exercise has an answer which is obvious, yet so easy to overlook. Allow yourself a maximum of 30 seconds to do the exercise.

Exercise #8-1 - Winning By Being The Slowest

A rather eccentric businessman wants to bequeath his financial empire and personal wealth to one of his two sons. He decides that a horse race will be run by the two sons. The son who owns the slower horse will become the owner of everything. Each son fears that the other will cheat by having his horse go slower than it is capable of going. Both of the sons approach a wise old philosopher for his advice. The philosopher, without much delay, tells them in two words how to make sure that the race will be fair. What are the two words.

If you were one of the two sons, is there something else you could have done to ensure you won the empire.

"WHY DIDN'T I THINK OF THAT?"

Following are several examples of people in business who have profited by seeing the obvious.

* An Edmonton man at a self-serve service station one day was wondering why they didn't have disposable gloves for people who pour their own gas and invariably get their hands dirty or acquire the smell of gasoline on their hands. From this obvious solution to a problem, an idea was born. Produce disposable gloves for the service station market. This is one of those obvious ideas that draws the "Why Didn't I Think Of That" comments. Overlooking the obvious is common in business. There are many "Why Didn't I Think Of That" stories.

* Danny Crowell of the Westin Hotel Chain came to one of our business decision-making classes to talk about innovation in the hotel industry. He told us about how their restaurant was able to increase the breakfast checks by an average of $2.50. The waitresses and waiters walked around with an orange juice container along with the coffee pots. Customers who would normally not order orange juice with their breakfast did so when they saw the tempting container of freshly squeezed orange juice. This was one of those ideas that is obvious but most people would not come up with.

* Morris E. Lasky's business is turning around money-losing hotels and resorts. Over the last thirty years he has saved over 100 hotels from financial ruin. The formula that Lasky uses is simple and quick. First he finds out what is wrong with the hotel or resort. Then he corrects it. How does Lasky find out what is wrong with the hotel? He does the obvious. He asks all the employess who work at the hotel. Ninety five per cent of the bailout plan comes from the employees' comments. The previous managers of these hotels could not see the obvious way to come up with a bail-out plan. Get the employees involved and ask them for what they know about what is wrong.

* When Tom Peters and Bob Waterman were investigating companies for their book "In Search Of Excellence", they were trying to find the key to success. The secret they were looking for was what made companies in America extremely successful. After several months of research, they were embarrassed to find out what the key was. It was the obvious. Companies which were successful did what they should be doing. They truly served the customer to death. This was no big surprise.

* Des Rice, of Mississauga, Ont. is known as the Weed Man. He has franchised over 84 lawn-care firms across Canada. The most important pieces of equipment are the sprayers. Having been a success in this business, he was looking for another business. He thought about it for years before it hit him. THE OBVIOUS. "And then according to colleague Tony Walton, it came, almost in a flash: "The question was, what can we spray and franchise that people will want to buy? Then we looked up, and there was the answer-windows!" The rest is history. He now franchises Blue Diamond Window Cleaning using power sprayers.

* In the 1800's bicycle manufacturers overlooked the obvious solution for years. The design of the bicycle first featured two wheels the same size but over time the front wheel got larger and larger. Initially the pedal assembly was attached directly on the front wheel. To make bicycles faster, the front wheel had to be increased in size. The problem was bicycles became rather cumbersome. The solution to this problem was before the industry's eyes. One day someone noticed something that was used in the manufacturing process of bicycles that could be used on the bicycles as well. It was a drive train assembly. This person thought why not use it to power the rear wheel. It was a matter of time before the bicycle was made with two wheels the same size.

MORE EXERCISES ON THE OBVIOUS

Exercise #8-2 - Matching Socks In The Dark

Five months ago a man threw away all his old socks and purchased 10 pairs of identical black socks and 4 pairs of identical brown socks. Since then he has lost 3 of the black socks and 1 brown sock. Assume there is a power failure in the evening just as he is about to go out. He is fully dressed except he does not have on his socks and shoes.

Unable to see in the darkness of his bedroom, what is the minimum number of socks the man has to remove from his dresser drawer to ensure that he has a matching pair?

Exercise #8-3 - The Obvious On The Typewriter Keyboard

Q W E R T Y U I O P

As you may already know, the above is the top row of the Typewriter keyboard. First here is some trivia about the typewriter; the layout of the keyboard was designed in the 1800's to slow typists down because they were jamming up the mechanical keys when typing too fast. We have more efficient keyboards which are compatible to the faster electronic typewriters. People have not accepted the new layouts because of resistance to change, another block to creativity and innovation.

So much for the trivia. What is the longest word that you can make in the English language with the top row of the typewriter keyboard.

Exercise #8-4 - Finding The Fastest Way

As President of Superior Time Air, you have just had a hectic week trying to get a number of projects completed. Time Air has regular scheduled flights to about 20 percent of the cities in Canada and United States. One of the projects involves your Charter Holiday Service. This is a new service just introduced to serve all of North America.

Your airline has just had 15,000 brochures printed which are slated to be put in travel agencies in all major cities across North America. You are trying to figure the fastest way for you to get these brochures out to all the agents. The peak holiday season is about to start and every minute counts.

Being a creative manager, how are you going to get these brochures to their destinations in the fastest possible time?

Exercise 8-5 - Dressing For Success

A bank in the U.S. realized that it needed to improve its image. One of the problems that needed attention was getting the employees to dress better. The bank was very concerned with what the reaction of the employees would be if a dress code was imposed by senior management. The bank management was able to resolve the problem with little resistance from the employees. How do you think they did it?

Exercise 8-6 - Why Aren't They Having Any Fun?

As the new manager of community facilities in a large city, you have noticed that children are not playing in the playgrounds. Someone has told you that children find playgrounds boring. What can you do about this problem?

Chapter 8 Notes

Exercises

#8-1

The two words are "Change horses" For the second part of the exercise, you could have shot your horse to make it the slowest.

#8-2

The man only need take out 3 socks to ensure he has a matching pair.

#8-3

Don't overlook the obvious. Try the word "Typewriter".

#8-4

As President of the airline you should practise one of the most fundamental principles of management: DELEGATE - to the head of the mailroom or the person in charge of these types of tasks.

#8-5

The policy of a new dress code was enthusiastically received by the employees of Security Financial Banking and Savings in St Cloud, Minn. because senior management "gave the problem away" to the employees. Instead of dictating a policy themselves, management named a committee of employees to come up with a policy. The committee proposed a dress code after their research. (As reported in Success, June 1988).

#8-6

You should get children involved in the design of your playgrounds.

CHAPTER 9

The Art Of Seeing Double Or Better

"Wise men learn more from fools than fools learn from wise men."

- Cato

"He who is not busy being born is busy dying."

- Bob Dylan

NON-LINEAR (LATERAL) THINKING

Most of us have a tendency to structure our thinking patterns in ways which prevent us from seeing all the possibility there is for finding solutions to life's problems. This tendency has a great impact on our creative abilities.

Test your flexibility in thinking with the following two exercises:

Exercise #9-1 - What Is Going On Here?

A 42 year old woman, a school teacher, bought her 6 year old daughter, Milisa, a new bicycle for her 6th birthday. On this day Milisa was riding the bicycle in front of an office building when she was struck by a car and injured. The police and ambulance were called and both arrived on the scene shortly after. The six year old girl was not injured seriously but the ambulance attendants decided to have her lie down on the stretcher so that she could be taken to the hospital for observation. Just as they were putting the little girl in the ambulance, a 28 year old clerk-typist ran out of the building and screamed "That's Milisa! What happened to my daughter?"

Whose daughter is Milisa, the school teacher's or the clerk-typist's?

Exercise #9-2 - Paper Clips For What?

You're the manager of a manufacturing company which by mistake made several million boxes of paper clips for which you have no market. These paper clips are now taking up valuable storage space. What alternatives do you have for disposing of the paper clips?

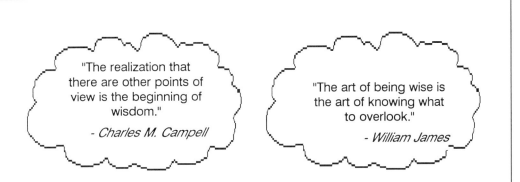

"The realization that there are other points of view is the beginning of wisdom."

- Charles M. Campell

"The art of being wise is the art of knowing what to overlook."

- William James

To find the most logical solution to Exercise #9-1, most of us require a breaking out of structured thinking patterns. In retrospect the solution is obvious. Yet the logical solution escapes many of us due to our set mind patterns.

Flexibility in thinking requires mainly effort on the thinker's part. Researchers have found that most successful people in business have developed the habit of thinking in flexible or non-linear terms. This results in innovative ways of marketing products, financing projects or managing employees.

Exercise #9-2 is not best solved with only linear or vertical thinking. Linear solutions are those which are rational and traditional. One linear solution is to sell the paper clips at the least possible financial loss? Vertical thinking is straight-forward thinking which involves careful logical analysis of the solution. Vertical thinkers will think only in terms of getting rid of the paper clips to organizations which want paper clips to clip papers together.

Non-linear thinking leads to more opportunites for a person in business than does linear or vertical thinking. Lateral thinking, a term coined by Edward de Bono, is another term for non-linear thinking. This mode to thinking goes beyond the rational and traditional.

A lateral thinker who attempts Exercise #9-2 will think not only in terms of disposing the paper clips to minimize losses, but also in terms of finding new uses for the paper clips. Lateral thinkers will explore all the different ways of using paper clips rather than just exploring the most logical and promising uses for them. Lateral thinking has to do with new ways of looking at things and generating new ideas of every sort imaginable. In my seminars we do an exercise to show that the uses for paper clips are literally unlimited.

Attempt solving the problem in Exercise #9-3 with lateral thinking.

Exercise #9-3 - The Flag Pole Dilemma

You are the manager of a McDowers hamburger outlet in the United States. McDowers is the largest chain of its kind in the world. Ray Block is the owner and demands excellence from his managers.

The time period is the late sixties. Four days ago a large riot resulted after a demonstration was held at Bent State University. The United States Army was called in to assist state police. In the confusion that resulted soldiers started shooting and killed four students. Anger and outrage have been expressed all over America, especially in universities and colleges.

After listening to the news on the radio, you drive into work and start your day. You work until noon and then take a break. Listening to the news on the radio you hear that marches are being held in all major cites and towns in the states and students are demanding all American flags be flown at half mast. You think about the flag pole in front of your McDowers outlet and the American flag on it. It occurs to you that it is a good thing no marchers are in front of your establishment. Ray Block, your boss, would think it unpatriotic to fly the flag at half mast because of an act the soldiers committed in the line of duty.

In fact, you know that Mr. Block would fire you if he knew that you bowed to the students' demands and flew your flag at half-mast.

At 2:00 o'clock in the afternoon, your assistant informs you that, a quarter of a mile away, there are 2,000 students on their way to your hamburger outlet demanding that you show your respect for the deceased. They want you to personally go out and lower the flag to half-mast. Television news crews and newspaper reporters are accompanying the angry students.

At this point you become very clear that if you do not lower the flag, the students will probably destroy a good part of your building. Ray Block will not be too happy about this. It is likely he will fire you if this happens. On the other hand he will probably fire you if you personally lower the flag since in his opinion this would be unpatriotic.

What will be your course of action?

This works a lot better than "PRIVATE BEACH, NO SWIMMING"

Exercise #9-3 is based upon a real life situation to which a manager had to react. If your decision was either to lower the flag for the students or to refuse to do so and suffer the consequences of having property damaged, your decision was based on vertical thinking. Lateral thinking was used by the manager who faced this situation in real life (see Chapter notes). His response saved him his job. There are several non-linear solutions to this situation. Can you come up with at least three original ones.

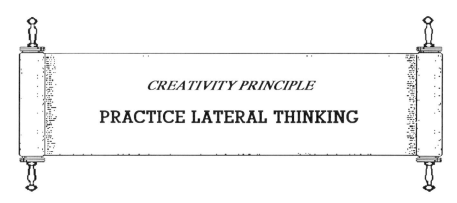

CREATIVITY PRINCIPLE

PRACTICE LATERAL THINKING

So remember to move your thoughts from being rigid and focused to a state of being different and interesting. Exercises #9-4 and #9-5 provide further practice in lateral thinking. Be sure to look for ideas which stem from the non-linear approach as well as the linear approach.

Exercise #9-4 - Queen Of Stones

Once upon a time, there lived a widowed queen who was selfish, jealous and ugly. She had a beautiful daughter who was loved by a young handsome prince. The princess was in love with the prince as much as the prince was in love with her. They decided to get married but had to get permission from the queen.

The queen also fancied the prince and wanted to marry him. So wealthy was the queen that her garden path was littered with diamonds and rubies. She was willing to give all her wealth to the prince if the prince married her; however, the prince only wanted the princess.

One fine afternoon while the three of them were strolling along the garden path, the queen proposed that they let chance decide who shall marry the prince. She stated that she would choose a ruby and a diamond from the path and put them in a jewelry box. Without looking, the princess would have to pick one of the precious stones from the box. If she chose the diamond the queen would marry the prince and if she chose the ruby the princess would be the lucky one to marry the prince.

The young prince and the princess reluctantly consented to this proposal. As the queen stooped to pick up two stones, the princess noticed that the unscrupulous queen selected two diamonds instead of a ruby and a diamond and placed them in the jewelry box. She then asked the princess to choose one of the two stones from the box without looking.

What should the princess do under the circumstances?

Exercise #9-5 - Case Of Health Cola, The Dental Pop

You are the marketing manager of Poco-Cola, the largest manufacturer and seller of cola in North America. Your rival has always been Cepsi-Cola which is a close second in the cola wars. After many years you are still fighting it out for market share. The fights have been fierce and will continue to be. You work 12 hours a day, six days a week trying to outguess what Cepsi-Cola is going to do. Last year you held 42% of the cola market and Cepsi held 38%. The remaining 22% was held by Ding-Cola (10%) and a number of smaller companies.

One of your assistant managers has just brought to your attention the market share figures for this year. Your company has slipped to 41% and Cepsi has gone up to 39%. This is bad news. There is another surprising fact. Health-Cola, an entry into the market just last year, has already captured 8% of the market. Industry specialists estimate that Health-Cola's share of the market will rise to about 12% this year with an outside chance of reaching as high as 20%. You had not paid any attention to Health-Cola because you thought it would flop. Now you are interested in more information.

You learn this about Health-Cola. It has a complex nucleic acid that imparts a sense of physical and emotional well-being. It has many vitamins and is sugar free and caffeine free. It also fights tooth decay. The Dental Association has approved Health-Cola as the cola to drink. Ken Johnstone, the Canadian runner who holds the world record, has appeared on many commercials for Health-Cola. Trendy's, the second largest hamburger chain in North America, just last week dropped your cola from their menu and replaced it with Health-Cola.

The last bit of information is a bit disconcerting. Your research people attempted to use the nucleic acid as well as other minerals to come up with a tooth-decay fighting cola. The attempts were a failure since your product tasted awful. Your researchers concluded that Health-Cola's fine taste was due to some secret combination of ingredients.

What are you going to do to respond to your loss of the market share?

THINKING LATERALLY IN BUSINESS

Great leaders in business regularly use lateral or non-linear thinking in their decision making. Many experts in the management field claim that the use or the lack of use of divergent thinking separates successful managers from the less successful ones.

We all can develop the ability to be more innovative and divergent in our thinking. The payoffs can be big. Here are just a few examples of the payoffs enjoyed as a result of lateral thinking used by business leaders.

Jan Carlzon in 1981 became president of Scandinavian Airline Systems (SAS) which was losing $17 million per year. After one year SAS was earning $54 million. What did Jan Carlzon do? He turned the organizational chart upside down and put those who dealt directly with the customer in charge of the airline. The traditional hierarchy was disbanded. Carlzon put those employees who served the customer on top. All others, including the CEO, were given the responsibility of serving those who serve the customers.

Stew Leonard runs a dairy store in Norwalk, Connecticut. His per-square-foot sales are 10 times the industry average. To most people food shopping is a bore. Not so for Stew Leonard's customers. Stew used lateral thinking and decided to add things in his store that would make people say "WOW". In the store you will find a petting zoo for children, a mechanical chicken in the egg department (world's fastest egg layer), and on one wall in the store, five thousand pictures of Stew's customers proudly displaying Stew Leonard's shopping bags.

Grant Lovig sells tons of cookbooks because he practices lateral thinking. Would you consider selling cookbooks in gas stations? Company's Coming Cookbooks are Canada's most successful series of cookbooks having sold over 4,000,000. Grant, the Vice-President of the company, used lateral thinking when he decided to market the cookbooks in service stations. Over 700,000 cookbooks were sold through a promotional program with Turbo Resources. In fact over 70% of Company's Coming's sales are through non-tradional avenues.

Gary Dahl who invented the Pet Rock was originally planning to market only a book on how to care for Pet Rocks. It occurred to him that if he marketed only the book, his book would be one of hundreds of thousands of books being sold. He decided he needed an edge. Out of his lateral thinking was born the actul Pet Rock. The addition of a rock being sold with a book made his product unique and consequently very successful.

Barry Kukes of Compu-Pak Inc. increased his sales of floppy diskettes 100% in just 5 months to an annual rate of 2 million dollars. How did he do it? By using "new" and "different" packaging. His first hit was the "Swimsuit" floppy diskette which featured a bikini-clad woman on the label. He came up with puppy dog labels and intends to use cars along with some other objects featured in the packaging.

Kukes is not worrying if his packaging does not make any sense. "What does a girl in a swimsuit have to do with a floppy diskette?" you ask. His answer: "We'll be the first to admit: absolutely nothing".

MIND BENDERS

Puzzles force us to think in new ways by challenging the way we think about ideas, numbers, shapes and words. Try these mind benders to practice your lateral thinking.

MIND BENDER #1 - What Is Brian Up To Now

The Prime Minister of Canada has just about completed remodelling the outside of his residence in Ottawa. He still needs something to finish the job. He goes down to the hardware store and looks at some items. If he buys these items, 1 will cost him $2.99 and 10 will cost him $5.98. Based on this he decided to buy 24.

The clerk charged the him $5.98 for 24. What did the Prime Minister buy?

MIND BENDER #2 - Half Of Thirteen Is Not Always 6.5

Use your flexibility in thinking to generate at least seven solutions to "What Is Half Of Thirteen?"

MIND BENDER #3 - Living With No Hope

An American businessman was captured by terrorists who wanted to get some ransom money in exchange for his release. No one wanted to put up the ransom money so they told him they were going to kill him. However, they told him that since he was a likeable guy, they would give him the choice of how he was to die. "If you tell a lie, you will be shot. Telling the truth will get you hanged."

The businessman made one statement. Based on this statement the terrorists set him free. What was the statement?

MIND BENDER # 4

What is the farthest a dog owned by a yuppie can run into the woods?

MIND BENDER #5

A child goes to the store with two coins which add up to 30 cents. One of the coins is not a nickel. What are the two coins that the child has?

MIND BENDER #6

Seven months of the year have 31 days. How many have 30 days?

MIND BENDER #7

Can you think of three different words which become smaller if you add letters to them.

MIND BENDER # 8

Anthropologists on an excavating expedition were looking for artifacts when one of the junior members excitedly yelled that he had found a gold coin marked 6 B.C. The leader of the expedition took one look at it and said it was not made in 6 B.C. The leader of the expedition, one not to tolerate stupidity, fired the junior member on the spot. Why?

MIND BENDER #9

A lady is celebrating her 10th birthday. On the same day her daughter who is 20 is getting married. How can this be?

REBUS MIND BENDERS

Can you determine what the following rebus stand for.

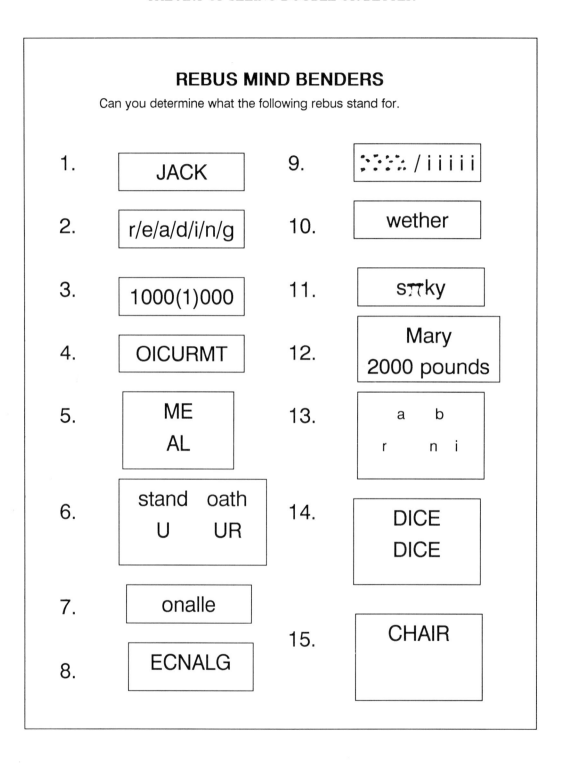

1. JACK

2. r/e/a/d/i/n/g

3. 1000(1)000

4. OICURMT

5. ME
   AL

6. stand oath
   U   UR

7. onalle

8. ECNALG

9. ⠒⠒⠒⠒ / i i i i i

10. wether

11. s⠒⠒ky

12. Mary
    2000 pounds

13. a   b
    r   n   i

14. DICE
    DICE

15. CHAIR

Chapter 9 Notes - Exercises

#9-1

Note how we easy it is for the majority of us to structure our thinking. (Only about 20% of seminar participants get this.) Milisa is the daughter of both the school teacher and the clerk-typist. The clerk-typist happens to be a man married to an older woman.

#9-2

This exercise is discussed in the Chapter content.

#9-3

There are many solutions available from lateral thinkers. One of my solutions was to delegate to an assistant manager and get lost. This way I would have some chance of retaining my job by claiming I was not around when the flag was lowered.

The manager who was actually faced with this situation knew that a nearby supplier was about to deliver some food supplies. The manager called the delivery man and told him to hurry over and knock down the flag pole with the delivery truck. The delivery man did this. The manager then phoned his boss and said the flag pole was knocked down by the delivery truck but he would have it back up the next day. He made no mention of the fact he had the flag pole intentionally knocked down.

#9-4

A normal type solution is for the princess to choose one stone and sacrifice her happiness. Another is to expose the queen's trickery.

One of the twenty or so good lateral solutions is for the princess to ask the queen to choose a stone and then say that since the queen chose a diamond the one remaining for the princess must be a ruby.

#9-5

One solution is the obvious, which is do nothing. You do not want to give Health Cola credibility by mentioning it in your advertisments. Cepsi may be your biggest concern, not health-cola.   (Continued on next page)

9-5 (Continued) I will mention only a few of the lateral solutions available to fight the problem of Health-Cola. One is to buy Health-Cola. Another is to buy the largest hamburger chain and feature your cola in all the outlets. You can also buy Trendy's, the second largest chain and drop health cola. Try getting an article published in a popular magazine about the ill effects of the ingredients of Health-Cola.

Mind Bender #1 - Hint: Brian Mulroney lives at #24 Sussex Drive.

Mind Bender #2 - Some solutions are one and three from 1/3, eleven (XI) and two (II) from XI/II, and four from thir/teen.

Mind Bender #3 - The man said "I want to be hanged" which was in essence a lie. This meant that they would shoot him. However this did not give the man his choice of death. Confused by this, the captors set him free.

Mind Bender #4 - Half way. The other half the dog runs out of the woods.

Mind Bender #5 - A nickel and a quarter make one of the coins not a nickel.

Mind Bender #6 - 11 (all except February).

Mind Bender #7 - Male, all, mall, small can become smaller. Also pig (piglet).

Mind Bender #8 - A coin marked 6 B.C. does not make any sense.

Mind Bender #9 - The lady was born on February 29 and is now 40 years old.

Rebus Mind Bender 1 - Jack in the box

Rebus Mind Bender 2 - Reading between the lines

Rebus Mind Bender 3 - One in a million

Rebus Mind Bender 4 - Oh I see you are empty

Rebus Mind Bender 5 - Square meal

Rebus Mind Bender 6 - You understand you are under oath

Rebus Mind Bender 7 - All in one

Rebus Mind Bender 8 - Backward glance

Rebus Mind Bender 9 - Specks before the eyes

Rebus Mind Bender 10 - A bad spell of the weather

Rebus Mind Bender 11 - Pie in the sky

Rebus Mind Bender 12 - Mary Overton

Rebus Mind Bender 13 - Scatter brain

Rebus Mind Bender 14 - Paradise

Rebus Mind Bender 15 - High chair

CHAPTER 10

Boy Are You Lucky You Have Problems

"I am an old man and have known a great many troubles, but most of them never happened."

- Mark Twain

"The thorns which I have reaped are of the tree I planted."

-Lord Byron

"I'll tell you, this whole world has gone bonkers. I was talking to my psychiatrist and he told me his psychiatrist has a lot of problems!"

PROBLEMS ARE LIFE'S OPPORTUNITIES

How do you view day-to-day problems? Do you always look at a big or complicated problem as an unpleasant situation? Well, you shouldn't. Creative people look at most complex problems as opportunities for growth. Each problem should be welcomed in your life as more opportunity to attain satisfaction. Our greatest satisfaction comes from solving complex problems.

Problems offer great opportunity in our lives if we want them to. Individuals and corporations will not only survive, but flourish in today's rapidly-changing world if they are good problem solvers. Good problem solvers are those who welcome problems and are challenged by them. The challenges start their creative juices flowing. The prescription for success in the modern world is the ability to enjoy and take advantage of problems.

Exercise #10-1 - As Easy As Rolling Off A Log

Assume you have a boss who is not very good with figures. In fact, your boss is the worst person who you know when it comes to math. Whenever your boss has a mathematical calculation to do, he comes to see you. Today he wants you to calculate the following equation for him.

$$123 + 456 - 23 = ?$$

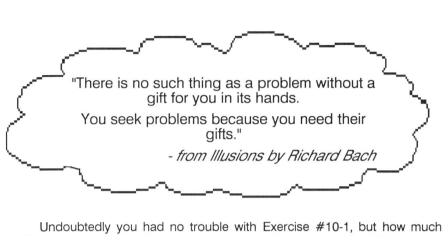

"There is no such thing as a problem without a gift for you in its hands.

You seek problems because you need their gifts."

- from Illusions by Richard Bach

Undoubtedly you had no trouble with Exercise #10-1, but how much satisfaction are you experiencing from having solved this problem? Unless you are as bad at math as your fictitious boss, you likely are not getting any satisfaction at all. Why not? Simply because there was not much challenge. If you had a job in which you were required to do elementary math calculations, no matter how high the pay, satisfaction attained would be nil.

Exercise #10-2 - A 5000 Year Old Puzzle To Solve

Now let's assume that your boss also likes puzzles. He is pretty good at puzzles but is stumped by one which he brings to you. This puzzle is about 5000 years old and was developed by the Chinese. Can you solve it?

If : = 6

 = 1

 = 3

What Does: Represent?

If you solved both exercises, which gave you more satisfaction? Obviously, the second did. This is a rather simple manifestation of how increasing the degree of difficulty in problem solving increases the amount of satisfaction. The point is that the bigger the problem, the greater the challenge. The greater the challenge, the more satisfaction that is experienced from solving the problem.

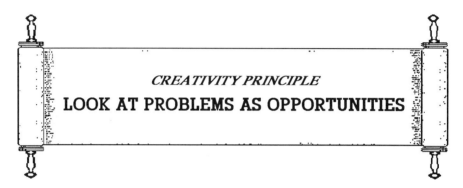

CREATIVITY PRINCIPLE

LOOK AT PROBLEMS AS OPPORTUNITIES

Being creative means welcoming problems as opportunities for attaining greater satisfaction in life. The next time you encounter a big problem at work, be conscious of your reactions. If you are self confident, you will experience a good feeling because you have another opportunity to test your creativity. For those of you who feel anxious, remember that you have the ability to be creative and solve problems. Any problem at hand is a great opportunity to generate innovative solutions and extract satisfaction from successfully solving the problem.

We all have two choices about problems. The first option is to resist the problem. This is somewhat ineffective. Resistance to problems stems from fear, laziness, or a lack of adequate time. Whatever the reason for the resistance, the problem will not go away. There is a rule of psychology which states that whatever we resist will persist. This is true with problems. Resistance will ensure the perpetuation of the problem.

The second option is for us to do something about the problem. We can draw on our abilities and take control. Highly-creative people actually get excited about a new problem because it means a new challenge. The new challenge eventually translates into a heightened state of satisfaction and growth. This occurs when the imminent solution is attained.

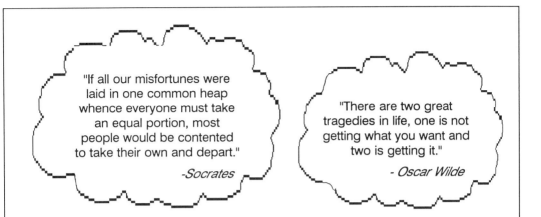

"If all our misfortunes were laid in one common heap whence everyone must take an equal portion, most people would be contented to take their own and depart."

-Socrates

"There are two great tragedies in life, one is not getting what you want and two is getting it."

- Oscar Wilde

THE GOOD, THE BAD, AND THE UGLY OF PROBLEMS

Many things have been said about problems and how we should handle them. The reality of problems can appear to range from the good to the bad to the ugly. Here are some points to think about. Whether the points are perceived as good, bad, or ugly will depend upon your interpretation.

1. Having a lot of money will not eliminate or reduce our problems. This is one fact that most people will not believe despite all the evidence in support of it. People want to believe that there is one big money deal in life that will take care of all their problems. This is believing in a form of Santa Claus; everything is going to be great once this saviour brings something of great value for us. Remember how false this belief was when we were children. Our happiness was short lived and our problems remained.

There is much more evidence before our eyes: The newspapers have thousands of stories about rich people who are in trouble with the law or have other major problems. A self-help group of lottery winners was formed in New York to deal with their serious depression which they had never experienced before their wins. A recent survey showed that a higher percentage of people making over $75,000 a year were dissatisfied with their incomes than of those making less than $75,000 a year. A larger percentage of the rich have alcohol and drug problems than the general population. The evidence is endless.

I have a theory about how well off we will be with a lot of money. If we are happy and handle problems well when we are making $25,000 a year then we will be happy and handle problems well when we have a lot more money. If we are unhappy and don't handle problems well on $25,000 a year then we can expect the same of ourselves with a lot of money. We will be just as unhappy and handle problems as ineffectively but with more comfort and style.

2. Successful people in business have more and bigger problems to handle than others less successful. The reason is that people who have what it takes to make money or run a large company handle and solve problems well. Consequently they are responsible for more and bigger problems. This is true of chief executive officers. A recent survey in Canadian Business Magazine reported that chief executive officers of Canada's largest corporations work an average of 11 hours a day. Evidently, these CEOs spend a lot of time solving many big problems. Millionaires claim that they still have problems, only more of them.

3. Certain problems can be given away. This is one of the most effective ways to solve problems. I had a problem in marketing my services because of the time required and because I liked doing other tasks better. This problem is one I gave away. I now have someone who likes doing my marketing for me. If you have a problem with a clerk in a post office who says it is impossible to send your package to a certain destination, the worst thing to do is to complain about the fact it can't be done. The clerk will become defensive and your problem will still be there. Instead give your problem away. Say to the clerk "Now what would you do if you were in my shoes." By giving your problem to the clerk you have increased the chances that he or she will find some creative way for getting the package to its destination. If you are a manager, you can give many of your problems away. How? By delegating of course. Think about problems you can get rid of by giving them to others. Then do it.

4. When we solve a problem, often it creates more problems. This has many variations. Our problem may be our not being married. Once we solve this by getting married, we then get to enjoy all the problems of marriage. Another problem may be our lack of enough clothes. Once solved we do not have not enough closet space and do not know what to wear. A problem of not having enough money when solved with a lottery win leads to many other problems such as old friends not having anything to do with us.

5. Painful incidents or major personal setbacks are often opportunites for creative growth and transformation. Many individuals report that their going through a divorce or losing the whole wad in Las Vegas can give the mind a good rattling. The result is an experience of creative awakening. Acts of failure such as not being promoted can result in a rebirth of creative thinking which had remained dormant for ages. Some people report that getting fired from a job was the best thing that ever happened to them. Major problems are mind shakers that break old habits of thinking.

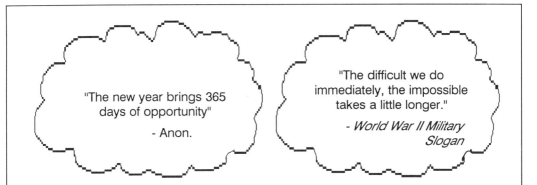

"The new year brings 365 days of opportunity"

- Anon.

"The difficult we do immediately, the impossible takes a little longer."

- *World War II Military Slogan*

5. A problem-free life is probably not worth living. If we were hooked up to a machine which did eveything for us we would eliminate all of our problems. It is likely not one of us will find this as an attractive substitute to life with its inherent problems. Yet people dream of a problem-free life.

6. If you want to get rid of your problems, just get yourself a bigger problem. Suppose you had a problem of deciding what to do this afternoon. As you were doing your pondering, a big mean grizzly bear started chasing you. The small problem of not knowing what to do will have been eliminated because of the bigger problem of the grizzly. The next time that you have a problem, create a bigger one to get rid of you first one. The smaller problem will be easily forgotten.

7. The best way to enjoy business problems is to be doing a job or running a company we really like. If we want to be master problem solvers, it is terribly important that we love our work. That means we should quit distasteful jobs. The best time to do it is now and we must forget the excuses for staying in situations which we do not relish. Finding work we like means we get to handle problems which we find enjoyable to solve.

8. Most problems can be transformed instantaneously just by changing the context in which we look at them. Why is it that some person can lose all of his millions of dollars and walk away saying "Big deal, it's only money, I still have me." Compare this to another well-off person who gets a five-dollar parking ticket and loses sleep over it for two nights. The difference is in the context in which the two look at problems.

It is not the reality or the degree of the problem, but the perceptual choice that determines how we view the seriousness of problems. We can change the quality of our lives just by choosing to change the context in which we view our problems. Context is about whether the glass is half empty or half full. Life works much better when we choose to see the glass as half full.

This Truckload Of Problems Can Make You Rich And Famous (see page 104)

OPPORTUNITIES IN PEOPLE'S PROBLEMS

People have millions of problems. These are our opportunities. The ability to spot and solve other people's problems can enrich our lives. Astute problem spotters and solvers are the shakers in business.

☆ Bette Nesmith Graham had a problem. She worked as a typist but made many typing errors. Bette knew that other typists had the same problem. Because of this, she founded a multi-million dollar industry. In the early fifties, IBM introduced their new electric typewriters with carbon film ribbons. When typists tried to erase typographical errors, a terrible mess was left behind on the paper. To overcome this problem Bette developed a white paint to use in correcting her typos. The paint worked well. She called it *"Liquid Paper"*. When Bette Graham offered IBM her new product, she was turned down. This problem was also an opportunity. She decided to market Liquid Paper herself. When Bette died in 1980, she was worth 50 million dollars.

Our careers or businesses depend on people's problems. All of our work involves some sort of problem solving. People will always have problems and we will always have many opportunites for solving these problems. Focusing on problems can make us rich and famous (if that is what we want). Even more important than wealth and fame is the satisfaction and enjoyment that comes from our effective solving of problems.

Exercise #10-3 - Focusing On Other's Problems

Identify five problems that others have in personal and business life. Then see if you can come up with some ideas on how to solve these problems by providing new products or services that people will buy.

Exercise #10-4 - Your Own Bug List For Fun Or Profit

Think about this. What bugs you? What bugs other people? Choose two "big" bugs and dream up of services or products that will help eliminate these bugs.

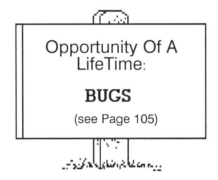

Opportunity Of A LifeTime:

BUGS

(see Page 105)

THE PROBLEM CUSTOMER IS AN OPPORTUNITY

When it comes to customers, we must remember the bigger the problem the bigger the opportunity. Most of us work in the service industry where "delighting" the customer is important for being highly successful. One of the biggest problems is that of the irate customer. This is the person who wants to create a scene and lets everyone else around know about his or her complaints (actually, I am one of these people). Many service employees perceive this person as an undesirable, someone to get rid of quickly.

The irate customer is actually a great opportunity. The successful handling of the problem can translate into some free advertising. If you can handle the irate customer's complaints to his or her satisfaction, he or she will become loyal to your business and will likely tell many people about your organization. Anyone this vocal will be a great source of word-of-mouth advertising.

PEOPLE PROBLEMS RIPE FOR BUSINESS OPPORTUNITES

1. Need for cleaner water
2. People unable to enjoy themselves
3. Cities are not friendly places
4. Need to conserve energy resources
5. Older people want to work longer.
6. Too many stray dogs and cats
7. Need for creative leisure programs
8. Resort areas are too expensive
9. Schools do not teach creative thinking
10. Businesses want to improve communication
11. Need for more humanistic work
12. Cheaper housing is required
13. Vacant space not rented out.
14. Companies are expensive to run
15. Many good products are not marketed effectively
16. Cheaper day care is desired
17. Better quality day care is required
18. Work is too boring
19. How to overcome illiteracy
20. Businesses are going bankrupt
21. How to make people aware of the hunger problem
22. Quality of education is too low
23. Too many young adults are dropping out of schools
24. How to trace children who have disappeared
25. How to make retirement meaningful
26. How to enrich marraiges
27. People are lonely
28. How to prevent suicides
29. People need a sense of community in their lifes
30. Increase the availability of information
31. Information overload
32. People do not know how to take responsibility
33. People want to make a difference
34. How to improve self-esteem
35. Many products lack quality
36. How to find the right job
37. How to meet new people
38. How to become self-actualized
39. How to spend money prudently
40. How to be happier in life
41. How to have power
42. How to attract funding for community and social programs
43. How to reduce stress
44. How to stay healthy
45. Too expensive vacations
46. How to deal with nagging relatives and in-laws
47. There are too many choices in life
48. Not enough time to get everything accomplished
49. People are afraid of crime
50. How to enlarge this list to 100 items

PEOPLE'S BUG LIST:

OPPORTUNITIES FOR NEW PRODUCTS AND SERVICES

1. too much news on the radio
2. having to lick stamps
3. telephone solicitors
4. negative people
5. overly-positive people
6. cigarette smoke
7. noisy clocks
8. too many signs on the streets
9. potholes on the road
10. polishing shoes
11. shaving
12. terrible books
13. shoe laces that break
14. dripping faucets
15. collection agents
16. having to take a car to a repair shop
17. relatives
18. insecure show-off yuppies
19. burnt out lightbulbs
20. having to buy a christmas tree
21. newspapers with negative news
22. having to write letters
23. not knowing what to write in letters
24. boredom with life
25. government red tape
26. big bunches of keys
27. yappy dogs
28. bad service in retail outlets
29. products that don't work
30. cars parked in front of your house
31. dents on your car when in parking lots
32. people taking up two parking stalls
33. people who drive too fast
34. soap dishes that you can't get the soap out of
35. having to write an essay, article, book, resume, etc.
36. two for one pizza of which even one isn't worth eating
37. shoe heels that wear out
38. shoes that never feel broken in
39. one good stocking left.
40. junk mail
41. small bathtubs
42. mowing lawns
43. noisy parties next door
44. having to wait in line ups
45. members of the opposite sex who come on too strong
46. too much advertising on T.V. and in magazines
47. offensive T.V. commercials
48. cafeteria food tasting like paper
49. having to deal with obnoxious people
50. long lists like this one

Chapter 10 Notes

Exercises

#10-1

I recommend a refresher course in math.

#10-2

The answer is 4.

By looking at the first three sets of three lines we can determine a pattern. The first line of the three represents 1, the second represents 2 and the third represents 4. If any of these lines is broken, then the line represents zero. The sum of the three lines represents the number. Therefore the one in question is:

$$0 + 0 + 4 = 4$$

CHAPTER 11

How To Be A Successful Failure

"The only thing we have to
fear is fear itself."

- Franklin D. Roosevelt

"The only thing we have to
fear is fear itself and possibly
the boogey man."

- Pat Paulsen

"The way to double your
success rate is to double
your failure rate."

*- Tom Watson (former
President of IBM)*

"Yes, I have been wrong before. As a matter of fact I made two errors in 1988 - same mistake both times. Twice I thought I was wrong but both times the error was that I was actually right."

Exercise #11-1 - Name This Man

Twice this person failed in business. He ran for State Legislature and didn't make it. Two times he lost in his bid for Congress. He did no better in the Senate races; twice he was defeated. Success eluded him when he worked hard to become Vice President of the United States. The woman he loved died when she was very young. Eventually this man suffered a nervous breakdown.

Who was this man?

Exercise #11-2 - The Key To Business Success

What is the most important quality, above all else, that chief executives and entrepreneurs have that help them achieve their success?

"A lot of disappointed people have been left standing on the street corner waiting for the bus marked Perfection".

- Donald Kennedy

"In order to get to the fruit of the tree, you have to go out on a limb."

- Shirley MacLaine

THE SUCCESS ROAD IS PAVED WITH FAILURE

The last chapter stressed that problems are opportunities and the bigger the problem to solve, the greater satisfaction we will obtain from solving that problem. If this is the case, why do many people avoid certain problems more than they would avoid a pit-bull terrier with rabies? One of the biggest reasons is fear of failure.

Many people avoid the risk of failure not realizing that success usually comes after a lot of failure. Take the example of the man in Exercise #11-1. This man was none other than Abraham Lincoln. All of his "failure" happened before he became one of the most famous Presidents of the United States.

On one hand North American society is obsessed with attaining success. On the other hand most members of this society are afraid of failure and try to avoid it. The need for success and the desire to avoid failure are contradictory. Failure is just a necessary step to success. Most of the time you will have to experience many failures before you experience success. The road to success looks something like this:

Failure Failure Failure Failure Failure Failure SUCCESS

The road to most success is paved with failure; failure and nothing else. Yet many people attempt to avoid failure at all costs. The fear of failure is associated with other fears such as fear of being seen as a fool, fear of being criticized, fear of losing the respect of the group, and fear of losing financial security. Avoiding failure means avoiding success.

AFRAID OF BEING A FOOL IS FOOLISH

There is a thin line between genius and insanity, I have erased that line.

-Oscar Levant

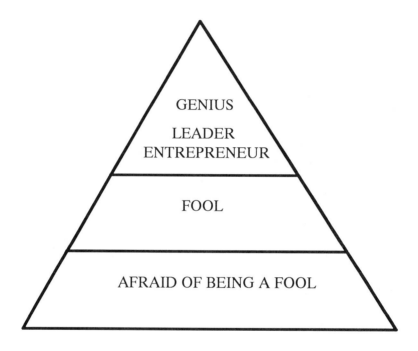

Many of us avoid taking risks because of our fear of looking bad if we fail. We get so obsessed with being liked that we will not do things which we feel may make us look bad in the eyes of others. Avoidance of risk becomes the norm. This can be very detrimental to our creativity and to our liviliness. We must learn to be fools if we are to be creative and live life to the fullest.

Afraid of being a fool is much worse than being a fool. Geniuses, effective leaders, and successful entrepreneurs have handled the fear of being a fool. They realize that in order to succeed in their endeavours they have to first be a fool; being foolish is essential to life's mastery. The point is that being "a fool" is on a much higher plane than being "afraid of being a fool" is. Life requires that we be fools now and then.

r + i - s = k

The above rebus stands for a calculated risk. Successful entrepreneurs and managers are good at taking risks. Seldom do they take outrageous risks. The risks they take are normally calculated to be reasonable so that the chances of winning are not so small as to be a stupid gamble and not so large as to be a sure thing. Today's leaders give themselves challenges which represent a reasonable probability of loss and a reasonable probability of gain.

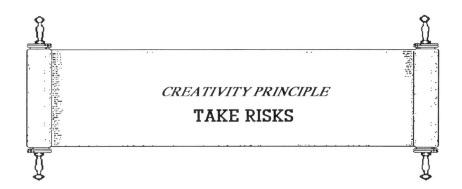

CREATIVITY PRINCIPLE

TAKE RISKS

THE KEY TO SUCCESS IS MANAGING FAILURE

Let us return to Exercise #11-2. There are many important factors for the success of entrepreneurs and managers. These include communication, vision, leadership, integrity, sensitivity, flexibility in thinking, confidence, courage, and constructive nonconformity. But the Centre for Creative Leadership in Greensboro, North Carolina found there was one factor that stood out more than the others. This is what gave achievers the final edge.

The biggest factor was their ability to manage failure. Successful people are not hindered or stopped by failure. They look at failure differently. They learn from it. In the end they actually welcome and celebrate failure.

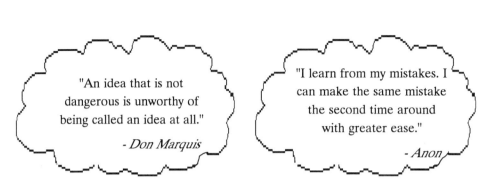

"An idea that is not dangerous is unworthy of being called an idea at all."
- *Don Marquis*

"I learn from my mistakes. I can make the same mistake the second time around with greater ease."
- *Anon*

RISKY BUSINESS VENTURES

With risk comes the probability of failure. That is the price we must be prepared to accept. The greater the risks, the greater the probability of loss. But with greater risks come bigger payoffs. Here are some people who risked.

☆ Thomas Edison is reported to have made several hundred experiments before he was successful in developing the lightbulb. After about 500 attempts, Edison's assistant asked him "Why do you persist in this folly? You have tried 500 times and you have failed 500 times." Edison was quick to respond "Oh but I have not failed even once. Now I know 500 ways of how not to make a lightbulb."

☆ Being a nonconformist at your job can be risky indeed. It can get you fired. Ask Tom Peters. He claims he was fired from Mckinsey & Co. Ask Lee Iacocca. He was fired from Ford Motor Co. Ask Stephen Jobs. He was fired from Apple Computers, the company he co-founded. Oh yes, ask me. I was fired from Edmonton Power. But I am in pretty good company with Peters, Iacocca, and Jobs. Can you say this? If you haven't been fired from a job, you may be too conservative.

☆ Peter Pocklington, the owner of the NHL Edmonton Oilers, took a big risk in the late 1970's when he purchased the rights to Wayne Gretzky and signed him to a seven year $1,500,000 contract. Of course this risk paid off when Gretzky developed into a great hockey player. Then Pocklington took another risk by selling Gretzky to Los Angeles Kings. Only time will tell if having taken this second risk pays off.

☆ An engineer who risked and lost over $1,000,000 for IBM is reported to have walked into Tom Watson's (former president of IBM) office and said "I guess you want my resignation". Watson replied " Why? We just spent over $1,000,000 million on your education.

WARNING TO POSITIVE THINKERS
SUCCESS OFTEN BREEDS FAILURE

"Positive thinkers" want us to believe that success almost always leads to more success. There is truth to success helping to create more success. It builds confidence in individuals and organizations. In addition, many new techniques and principles are learned on the way to success. These are usually helpful in attaining more success in future endeavours.

What "positive thinkers" often do not point out is nothing breeds failure like success. More often than is acknowledged, success leads to failure. There are two major reasons for this. The first one is the law of averages. On the average, we have way more unsuccessful endeavers than successful ones. The odds for failure are much greater than for success, even just after being successful.

The second reason for success leading right into failure relates to ego and complacency. Organizations and individuals who make it big usually get fat heads. They tend to think they have the solution and now they know it all. Nothing can be further from the truth. No matter how successful a product, service or technique is, it will not be the right one for all circumstances. As we know, circumstances have a tendency to change. When circumstances change abruptly, many organizations and individuals are faced with a product, service, or technique that no longer serves its purpose well. The organization or individual is not able to adequately respond to the new business climate. Tough times follow.

Entrepreneurs have been known to build highly successful companies and then find themselves in deep financial trouble. What sometimes happens is entrepreneurs, men more so than women, want to show the world they have arrived. They buy a big house, an expensive car, and a host of other items. Money is siphoned out of the business just when the business becomes highly successful. The problem here is that competitors usually move in when they see a business making it big in a certain industry. This is when the successful business requires a large amount of money to deal with the competition. If it does not, the once successful company soon finds itself in deep financial trouble. Success then leads to failure.

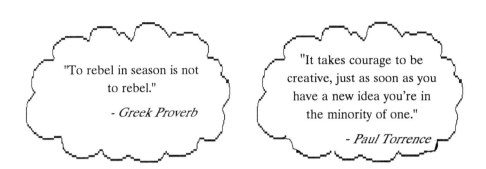

"To rebel in season is not to rebel."

- Greek Proverb

"It takes courage to be creative, just as soon as you have a new idea you're in the minority of one."

- Paul Torrence

HOW TO MAKE A DIFFERENCE

Exercise #11-3 - A Common Trait In Uncommon People

What did the following people have in common?

* Mother Teresa
* Thomas Edison
* Albert Einstein
* John F. Kennedy
* Gandhi

What is the best way to make a big difference in this world? Answer: *Start off by being different.* Being creative is thinking something different. It is also being different than most people. We must diverge from the norm to generate something new and worthwhile. This will take courage since people who diverge from the norm are frowned upon. We must dare to be different if we are to achieve anything of major importance.

When you want your life to be interesting and exciting, be different. Be different than you normally are and be different than the majority of people in your life. One warning must be given here. You will not get much support from your friends, co-workers, or society when you take the step to be different. They will certainly not encourage you to stand out.

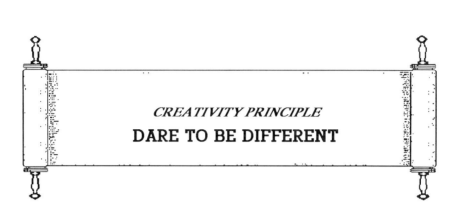

CREATIVITY PRINCIPLE

DARE TO BE DIFFERENT

Your motivation to be different has to come from within. The motivation should come from the realization that anything of major consequence in this world was probably initiated by someone who was different than the rest of society. In fact they were probably out of step with society to a large degree.

Just think about the individuals in Exercise #11-3. Thomas Edison, Albert Einstein, Mother Teresa, Gandhi, and John F. Kennedy made a big difference. What they have in common is that they are or were different than the majority. They were out of step. None of these people were conformists.

The point is that being an achiever means being different and feeling good about it. Some people may be uncomfortable with you and others may dislike you for it. You will be criticized a lot. The more success you have at being different, the more you may be disliked. But people will respect you for it, especially when you start making that big difference. You will also have your own respect.

Exercise #11-4

Write down how you are limiting yourself in your life by trying to be like everyone else so that you fit in and are accepted. What can you do to be different that will help you make a differnce? What will the consequences be?

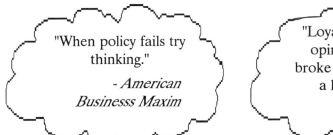

"When policy fails try thinking."

- American Business Maxim

"Loyalty to petrified opinion never yet broke a chain or freed a human soul."

- Mark Twain

RULES AND ASSUMPTIONS NOT TO LIVE BY

Being different means challenging the status quo. It is a good idea for individuals and organizations to constantly challenge rules and assumptions. Discarding outmoded rules and unproven assumptions throws a new perspective on business situations. Innovation tends to flow freer and performance of organizations improves.

Many rules, both written and unwritten, are outdated and serve absolutely no purpose. Often rules are followed without any thought to whether there is a purpose for them. Rules can hinder the generation of new ideas and impede the implementation of innovative ways of doing business.

For many years Canadian doctors and lawyers subjected themselves to a rule that restricted the advertising of their services. This rule interfered with their ability to tell the public about their being in business and the types of services they have to offer. Only after constant challenging of this rule by some of their members have these professionals come to grips with the obsolescence of this rule. Now more freedom in advertising is allowed.

We should constantly challenge not only rules but also assumptions. Our voices of judgment constantly make assumptions about the way things are. Often these assumptions have little or no relationship to the ways things are. Only through challenging of assumptions can we determine their validity.

Here is one example of a common erroneous assumption. Most managers still believe that money is the prime motivator of employees. If as managers we make the wrong assumption that all employees are motivated by money, our approach to management will be solely dictated by having employees compete for monetary incentives. This will be very ineffective. Researchers such as Herzberg have found that money is not at all the best motivator of employees. Instead recognition and room for growth are better motivators. Money as the prime motivator is only one of many wrong assumptions being made which hinder organizational effectiveness.

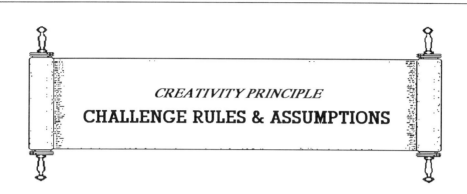

CREATIVITY PRINCIPLE
CHALLENGE RULES & ASSUMPTIONS

RULE BREAKERS WHO WERE REWARDED

Many businesses owe their success to their willingness to challenge prevailing assumptions and rules of their industry. Because most businesses in all industries do not have the presence of mind to challenge the status quo, a great deal of opportunity exists for the businesses and individuals who develop new methods by challenging assumptions and breaking rules.

If we look at any of today's highly-successful businesses, we will see businesses which are risking, being different, and challenging the rules. Following are a few examples of individuals and businesses which have profited from their willingness to challenge old ways of doing business.

The Backwards Rule Book Of Advertising

By Knot Thinking

☆ One of the written rules of business relates to how much advertising a business does. The guideline normally given by business textbooks is to follow the industry average which is calculated as a percentage of sales. The Brick Furniture chain during its rapid growth rate advertised at a level far exceeding the industry average. By challenging and breaking the rule that one's business should advertise in the area of the industry average, the Brick grew much faster than any of its competitors. Following the industry average has no relationship to the optimum level for any particular business. Another reason for not following the textbook recommended practice of tying advertising to a percentage of sales is that this practice is backwards. This approach results in large amounts of advertising being done when sales are high and small amounts being done when sales are low. The opposite should be done.

☆ I had the opportunity to visit a restaurant in Western Canada which decided to violate the unwritten industry rule that prices should be stated in the menu. This restaurant instead asked customers to pay what they thought the meals were worth. Most restaurant owners will say this is a stupid idea because customers will rip the owners off. Well, guess what? The customers actually paid about $2.00 per entree more than the owner would have charged with regular prices. A restaurant in Los Angeles using the same format reported customers paying $5.00 to $6.00 an entree more than was expected.

American Restaurante

Menu

Just Pay Us What You Think The Food Is Worth

Publishers' Erroneous Zones

(What Most Publishers Don't Know About Publishing)

☆ When he wanted to get his book published, Dr. Wayne Dyer was told by publishers that his writing skills were horrible and his book, *Your Erroneous Zones*, would not sell with his inadequate writing style. Dyer decided to stick with the way his book was written and eventually found a publisher. His book turned out to be one of the best selling non-fiction books of all time. Other authors such as Robert Ringer (author of *Winning Through Intimidation*) have similar stories to tell.

☆ The Calgary Flames hockey club in the 1980s is being touted as the one of the best in the NHL. Virtually all of the other NHL clubs have counted on the NHL draft of juniour hockey players to improve their clubs. The Flames management did something different. They signed American college hockey players who the other clubs regarded as unable to play in the NHL. Calgary Management also decided to build a good club using free agents instead of relying on the junior draft.

Breaking The Unwritten Rules In Hockey

By the Calgary Flames

APHORISMS TO MOTIVATE YOU TO RISK, CHALLENGE AND BE DIFFERENT

BEING OKAY

If you could really accept that you weren't okay, you could stop proving you were okay.

If you could stop proving that you were okay, you could get that it was okay not to be okay

If you could get that it was okay not to be okay, you could get that you are okay the way you are.

YOU'RE OKAY, GET IT!

- *Werner Erhard*

I would rather sit on a pumpkin, and have it all to myself, than be crowded on a velvet cushion.

- *Henry David Thoreau*

Conform and be dull

- *J. Frank Dobie*

The greatest test of courage on earth is to bear defeat without losing heart.

- *Anon*

If a million people say or do a stupid thing, it still remains a stupid thing.

- *Anon*

Someone who tries to do something and fails is a lot better off than the person who tries to do nothing and succeeds

-Anon

Be bold - and mighty forces will come to your aid.

- *Basil King*

119

Chapter 11 Notes

Exercises

#11-1

See page 109

#11-2

See page 111

CHAPTER 12

Creative Thinking Is An Exercise In Silliness

"Imagination was given to man to compensate him for what he is not. A sense of humour was provided to console him for what he is."

- Horace Walpole,

Man of Letters

"Life is much too important to be taken seriously"

- Oscar Wilde

Kilroy was not here!
- Clem

GROWING UP MAY BE HARMFUL TO HEALTH

The above figure is one of the mysterious "Clem" who originated in Britain and has appeared in thousands of washrooms across many nations. He has been mistaken for the legendary "Kilroy was here" which originated in United States and has also had great washroom presence. Over the years Kilroy's name has been combined with Clem's picture in North American washroom's. Most North Americans think Clem is Kilroy. Not so. Clem is Clem and Kilroy is Kilroy.

By now you are probably wondering what this story has to do with this book. Absolutely nothing. I just kind of like the story and I needed a creative way to get your attention for this section. I thought this would be a good time to be silly and unreasonable. Besides I always wanted to tell people this trivia about Clem and Kilroy that has absolutely no use to anyone.

Oscar Wilde said "Life is much too important to be taken seriously". How serious are you in life? Do you find time to laugh, play and be foolish? If you are always serious and trying to be reasonable, you are sabotaging your creativity. Individuals who are too serious to have fun rarely come up with something new and stunning.

Play is at the heart of creativity. Playing and having fun are great ways to stimulate our minds' abilities. When we are having fun, we tend to be relaxed and enthusiastic. Sometimes we even become outrageous. All of these states complement the creative spirit.

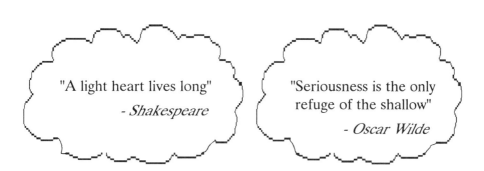

"A light heart lives long"
- *Shakespeare*

"Seriousness is the only refuge of the shallow"
- *Oscar Wilde*

Exercise #12-1 - Who Needs A Second Childhood?

Spend about two or three minutes thinking about someone you know who is a senior citizen (over 65) and is still very vibrant and active. List the qualities that this person has. Once you have listed the qualities think of what age group these qualities are characteristic of.

Some of the qualities respondants to the above exercise will list are enthusiastic, sense of humour, creative, spontaneous, playful, friendly, inquisitive, and joyful. Note that these are the qualities that children possess. In other words, people who are active and happy in their later years do not need a second childhood because they never gave up their first one.

Ever wonder why children are so creative? One of the important reasons is they know how to play and have fun. Remember when you were a child. When you were playing you were learning. You probably learned a lot more during your lighter moments than during your serious moments. Try and re-experience the child in you if you want to increase your creativity.

Creativity requires playfulness, daydreaming, and foolishness. These are the things society discourages us from being or doing. We are told to "grow up". We must be able to ignore what the majority in society wants us to be like. For us to be more innovative, we must learn new ways of playing with things, words, puzzles, ideas, and other people. We must never grow up; when we grow up, we stop growing.

HUMOR IS NO LAUGHING MATTER

In his early 90's George Burns started taking bookings for his 100th birthday. If he lives for more than a century, it will probably be because of the attitude he has carried through life. He has made a living out of humor. Undoubtedly, his health has benefited from his work. Researchers are finding that boisterous laughing many times a day will give you the same effects as a 10 mile run. Another man who benefited from laughter was Norman Cousins. Faced with what doctors diagnosed as a terminal illness, Cousins proved the medics wrong by watching reruns of Candid Camera and Groucho Marx films. He was able to laugh himself back to health.

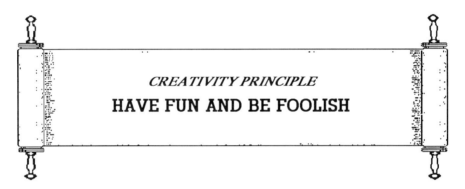

CREATIVITY PRINCIPLE
HAVE FUN AND BE FOOLISH

Besides being good for our health, humor is an effective way to promote creativity. Experts in creativity have observed that stunning solutions are often triggered by humor. Seriousness hinders the creative flow. When you are under a lot of stress and pressure or stuck in a serious state of mind, the best thing to do is to get out a joke book. Get together with someone who can laugh about anything. Fool around. You'll be surprised at the number of creative ideas that start to flow.

Several years ago a group of high school students were given a test in creativity. Two equal sub-groups were formed. One of the sub-groups enjoyed the half hour before the test by listening to a recording of a comedian. The other sub-group spent the half-hour in silence. When subjected to the test, the students in the first group did much better than the second group.

Comedy and laughing will open up your thinking. Laughing tends to make you look at things in unusual ways. This is because laughter changes your state of mind. There is little concern for being wrong or being practical. It is okay to be foolish. This fosters the flow of creative solutions.

Poking fun at work situations is one way of stimulating creativity. You are more apt to break the rules when poking fun at a problem. In a state of playing with the problem your defences are down and your mental locks released. This results in more innovative and exciting responses to the problem at hand. Managers should learn how to encourage their employees to poke fun at all important matters in the work place.

Exercise #12-2 - "Your Seriousness Deserves A Laugh"

Recall the most stressful situation you have had at work during the last few months. Try to find as many amusing things as you can think of about this situation. Poke fun at it. What outrageous things could you have done?

Did you come up with anything interesting? If you didn't, try discussing the situation with a friend who has a good sense of humor. Poke fun at the situation with your friend. You're bound to come up with some idea which is exciting and offers some promise for the next time a similar situation happens to you.

Exercise #12-3 - Your Company Is A Joke

Imagine that you are the General Manager of your company (if you aren't already). Now think of twenty foolish, outrageous, impractical, or humorous things you could do to make the company environment a place that people would be dying to work in. Let go all of your defences. Write all your ideas down. Then fully evaluate your ideas with the PMI method from Chapter 6 to see if there is any promise in any of them.

QUOTATIONS TO LIGHTEN YOUR MIND

"The report of my death was exaggerated."

- Mark Twain

"I never forget a face, but I'll make an exception in your case."

- Groucho Marx

"Of all my wifes relatives, I like me best."

- Anon

"A man is never drunk if he can lay on the floor without holding on."

- Joe E. Lewis

"All generalizations are dangerous, even this one."

- Alexander Dumas

"He has occasional flashes of silence that make his conversation perfectly delightful."

- Sidney Smith

"There is nothing you and I make so many blunders about, and the world so few, as the actual amount of our importance"

- Josh Billings

"I never travel without my diary. One should always have something sensational to read on the train."

- Oscar Wilde

"I like a woman with a head on her shoulders. I hate necks."

- Steve Martin

"If it wasn't for pickpockets, I wouldn't have any sex life at all."

- Rodney Dangerfield

"Don't stay away from church because there are so many hypocrites. There's always room for one more."

- Anon

Exercise #12-4 - Abbreviations To Have Fun With

Why not have some fun before your next important office meeting. Fun puts everyone in a better state of mind. One way is to play some game or do puzzles. The abbreviations below stand for relationships and associations which you should be aware of. Have fun with these before you make up your own. Then give them to your colleages to figure out before your next meeting.

Examples: 24H. = 1D. (24 Hours = 1 Day) N.N. = G.N. (No News = Good News)

1. 12 I. = 1 F.

2. B.M.W. + M.B. + P. = Y. C.

3. 4P. = E.

4. E. O. + T. M. L. + W. J. + M. C. + Q. N. = N. H. L. H. T.

5. F. D. was said by P. E. T.

6. 50 S. = U.S.A.

7. 10 D. = 1 C.

8. 1 + 3 Z. = 1 T.

9. L.A. + S.F. + S.D. are in C.

10. J. F. K. + R. N. + R. R. were P.

11. I. W. T. H. Y. H. was sung by the B.

12. J. + P. + R. + G. = T. B.

13. M. is in C. A.

14. 1 Y. + 1 D. = 11 Y.

15. M. J. sang with the R. S.

16. H. + W. + C. = F.

17. J. C. was born on C. D.

18. Y. + N. W. T. = N.C.

19. S. + 2 D. = M.

20. E. J. + N. I. + T. G. & M. + N. Y. T. + V. S. = N.

MORE GRAFFITI FROM THE NATIONS' WASHROOMS TO PROVIDE WISDOM AND OPEN UP YOUR CREATIVITY

With all the barriers to creativity in our society, many people find that the only place they get to be creative is in the washroom. A lot of the graffiti they write is highly creative. Here are another two pages of it. Please share these with your fellow workers before your next meeting. Your group's creativity may be opened up.

GOD IS DEAD

(Our God is alive; sorry to hear about yours)

58% of all deaths are fatal

There is a dance in this town every Saturday Night this week

What will you do when Jesus comes?

(Move Gretzky to right wing)

There is no such thing as Gravity. The earth sucks.

Lassie kills chickens

JESUS SAVES!

Even more than the Superstore?

The world ends at 10 tonight---details on the 11:00 o'clock news

Mary had a little lamb and boy was she surprised

My inferiority complexes are not as good as yours

1 bet you 1 could stop gambling

Dionne Quintupulets were a hoax - Five couples were charged in the conspiracy

Colonel Gaddafi buys USA Savings Bonds

An empty taxi stopped and Ronald Reagan got out

Orville was right

I'm not prejudiced. I hate everyone equally

TIME IS NATURE'S WAY OF KEEPING EVERYTHING FROM HAPPENING AT ONCE

I'm trying to arrange my life so that I don't even have to be present

Can a blue man sing the whites?

Twiggy is only skin deep

Alimony is like buying hay for a dead cow.

Kilroy Was Here!

I was not. - signed Kilroy

Mona Lisa was framed

Chicken Man has a Fowl mouth

If you do it in a MG, don't boast about your Triumphs

You're never alone with schizophrenia

Perforation is a rip off

Roget's Thesaurus dominates, regulates, rules, Ok, all right, adequately.

GOD LOVES YOU

(God won't love you for destroying someone's property by writing on it.)

Dyslexia lures, KO

Ben Johnson gave us the runaround

I love grils

(which was corrected thus:)

You mean girls stupid!

(but then corrected again)

What about us grils?

Arrange the following words into a well-known phrase or saying:

OFF PISS

I never used to be able finish anything, but now I.......

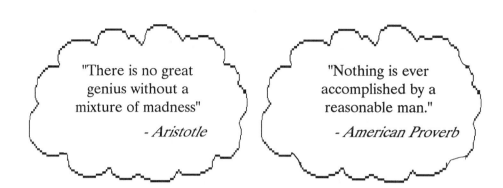

"There is no great genius without a mixture of madness"

- *Aristotle*

"Nothing is ever accomplished by a reasonable man."

- *American Proverb*

THERE IS REASON TO BE UNREASONABLE

Society and our educational institutions teach us to be reasonable and practical. Being reasonable and practical is a fine alternative if we are talking about not doing something stupid like jumping off a cliff. The problem is that society wants us to be "reasonable" in ways which hinder our creativity.

Just because the majority in society holds a belief, the belief is not necessarily true. What society considers reasonable may actually be very unreasonable. High numbers of people have held false beliefs before. Remember that nearly all of mankind at one time thought the world was flat. This statement made by Bertrand Russell offers much food for thought.

"The fact that an opinion has been widely held is no evidence whatever that it is not entirely absurd; indeed in view of the silliness of the majority of mankind, a widespread belief is more likely to be foolish than sensible."

Another philosopher, Albert Einstein, stated "Great spirits have always encountered violent opposition from mediocre minds". When we are considering something new and different, we do not have to look far to have someone tell us we are being unreasonable. We must be on guard and reject reason. Minding the reason of others has wrecked many peoples' plans.

If we are to create anything that makes a difference in this world, we must also learn to challenge our own reasonableness. Remember that our own voices of judgment can be an enemy of our plans. Our own reasons for not doing something should constantly be challenged if we are to succeed in our creative endeavors.

I personally have found that "being unreasonable" is something that can be done on a daily basis. When I encounter either my own voice of judgment or someone else's, I try to go against the prevailing reason. By being unreasonable, I find some surprising and rewarding events occur.

One time I decided to be unreasonable and go see a Professor who had given me a much lower mark than I thought I deserved on a mid-term paper. What made my going to see him unreasonable was that at least four other students in his class felt the same way about their marks and had already gone to see him. He became very defensive and refused to give any of them any consideration for a higher mark. My unreasonableness paid off. I was able to get consideration from him despite four other students having tried before me. I just did things a little differently. I did not make him wrong by saying that he graded my paper unfairly. Instead I said to him "I messed up my last paper which may cost me a good final mark in this course. What would you do if you were in my shoes?" He responded by reducing the weight of the mid-term paper and counting my final paper more. I wound up with honors in the course.

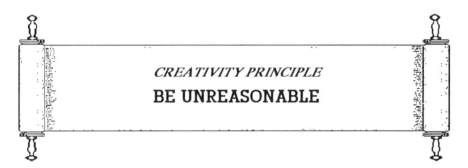

CREATIVITY PRINCIPLE

BE UNREASONABLE

Exercise #12-5 - Thinking About Being Unreasonable

List the areas in your life or work where you can be more unreasonable. Think about the times when you listen to other people's voices of judgment as well as your own. Define what steps you can take to see if something different happens than what you initially assume will happen.

Then make it a point of being unreasonable at least once a day.

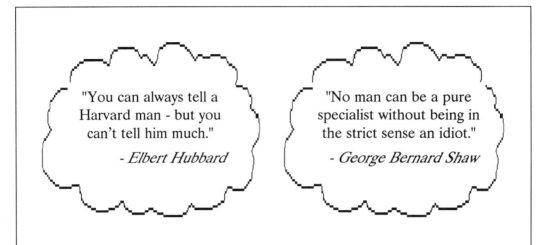

"You can always tell a Harvard man - but you can't tell him much."

- Elbert Hubbard

"No man can be a pure specialist without being in the strict sense an idiot."

- George Bernard Shaw

SPECIALIST'S DISEASE

Industry specialists are supposed to be people who we rely on for advice if we want to know anything about that industry. Specialists may be able to tell us what worked in the past; however, we should be careful about accepting their advice about what will work in the future. Researchers have found that the more specialists think they really "know" something, the less they are open to new approaches. This has been called "specialist's disease".

"Experts" in a particular industry may con us into believing that they know more than we do about their industry because they work in that industry. Apparently they are supposed to know what is reasonable and what isn't. Their beliefs can be liabilities. Rigid beliefs and unyielding thinking patterns have been known to stifle creativity in many fields. Elbert Hubbard defined a specialist as "one who limits himself to his chosen mode of ignorance".

My personal experiences have taught me to be wary of someone who tries to impress me with the validity of their knowledge of their industry based on how long they have been in their occupation. I have found out that often my best bet is to be "unreasonable" and not listen to the "experts." Instead I find out for myself what can be done and what cannot be done in that industry.

Remember that Christopher Columbus went against the belief of the times that the world was flat. Flat-world thinking exists today, only in different forms. There are "flat-world thinkers" in all industries. Some of the most important discoveries and inventions have resulted from people being totally unreasonable and defying the experts. Following are two examples.

☆ Developers of the jet aircraft had to contend with their industry's "flat-world thinkers". The United States National Academy of Sciences in 1940 issued a statement declaring that there would never be such a thing as a jet aircraft: "Even considering the improvements possible - the gas turbine could hardly be considered a feasible application to airplanes, mainly because of the difficulty of complying with the stringent weight requirements."

☆ In the late 1980s, two researchers, K. Alex Mueller and J. George Bednorz, at IBM disobeyed their bosses and launched a new industry by developing a practical way of creating superconductors. The incredible fact of this story is that they were not experts in this field. They worked with substances that the experts had considered to only have insulating properties and not conductivity potential. By disobeying their superiors and defying the experts, these two men won a Nobel Prize for science.

AIRLINE AVOIDS SPECIALISTS TO MAKE PROFIT

In 1981 British Airlines (BA) had losses of 1 billion dollars. Some people said BA stood for "bloody awful". Because British Airlines needed a new outlook to get back on its feet, John King, the Chairman, was looking for a new chief executive officer. To fight specialist's disease, he wanted to hire someone who was definitely not associated with the airlines industry. In other words this was the important qualification, no experience with an airline.

John King hired Colin Marshall who had worked in retail but never in airlines. King and Marshall transformed BA to the most profitable airline in the world in 1988. King reported that there seemed to be an advantage in not knowing too much about the business. He stated that in their ignorance, they could do things they might not have done if I they had been better informed.

WHAT IF WE ASK "WHAT IF" QUESTIONS

One of the best ways to practice being unreasonable is to ask random "what if" questions. These are questions that may sound absurd and unreasonable. Nonetheless, "what if's" can lead us to some interesting notions. Some examples of "what if" questions are:

- ☆ <u>What if</u> we marketed our product with something totally unrelated?
- ☆ <u>What if</u> we invited our top customers to our employee Christmas party?
- ☆ <u>What if</u> we asked our employees to buy our competitors' products and not our own?
- ☆ <u>What if</u> we made our product .... bigger, more colorful, more expensive, more stylish, etc.?
- ☆ <u>What if</u> we asked the customer to pay what the customer thought our product was worth in comparison to our competitors products?

Benefits Of "What If" Questions.

- ✓ First, we get the opportunity to explore certain possibilities that we would not otherwise do.
- ✓ Second, "what if" questions may lead us to ideas altogether different from the one we started with.
- ✓ Last, "what if" questions are a lot of fun.

Exercise #12-6 - "What If You Told The Boss To.......?

Ask yourself ten "what if" questions about your job. See if you can generate some new ideas about how to improve the job.

CHAPTER 13

Zen There Was
The Now

"Oh, to reach the point of
death, and realize one has
not lived at all"

-Thoreau

"This time, like all times, is a
very good one, if we but
know what to do with it."

-Ralph Waldo Emerson

Lost

Yesterday, somewhere between sunrise and sunset, two golden hours, each set with sixty diamond minutes. No reward is offered, for they are gone forever.

- *Horace Mann*

Exercise #13-1 - The Three Secrets To Fulfillment

A North American entrepreneur had acquired a lot of material wealth but was still not happy in life. He heard about a Zen master living in the far east on a mountain that was hard to find. This Zen master knew three important secrets about how to live life to the fullest. The entrepreneur heard that anyone who had found out these three secrets and had followed them ended up living a happy, fulfilling life.

Because his life was so empty and often dejecting, the entrepreneur decided to go in search of this Zen master. He felt he needed to know what the three secrets were so he could start living life to the fullest. After twenty months of searching, the entrepreneur finally found this Zen master high on top of an obscure mountain.

The Zen master was happy to reveal the three secrets to having a happy and satisfying life. The entrepreneur was surprised at what he was told. What do you think the three secrets were?

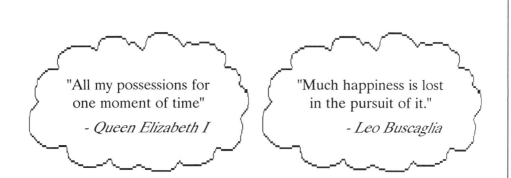

"All my possessions for one moment of time"

- Queen Elizabeth I

"Much happiness is lost in the pursuit of it."

- Leo Buscaglia

NOW WE HAVE THE NOW

At a Safeway store I frequent there are two express cashouts with one of the cashout counters being closer to the exit than the other one. Long ago I became facinated by the number of people who are in a hurry, yet are totally unconscious about the fastest way to get out of the store. Many customers will get in the lineup that has the most people. This lineup looks more appealing because the cashout counter is closer to the exit of the building. These people do not pay attention. They do not see that the second express, which is next to the first one but farther from the exit, will be faster because there are anywhere from one to five fewer people in it.

Someone once said that 95% of the people are unconscious 95% of the time. After seeing many situations similar to the above situation in the Safeway store, I wonder if this person is not right. It appears to me that most people are not in the present moment very often. This is very unfortunate since they miss out on many opportunities in life. Of course the fact they are that way is somewhat fortunate for people who choose to be conscious. For example, I get in the short line in Safeway and am well on my merry way while others who arrived at the checkouts ahead of me are waiting impatiently for their line to move.

Having a presence of mind or paying attention to the moment is something most of us can improve upon and benefit from. The ability to be in the now and concentrate on the task at hand is a very important aspect of the creative process. Being in the now is emphasized in Zen, an Eastern discipline, which has personal enlightenment as its goal. Following is a story told in Zen teachings.

The Muddy Road - A Zen Story

Two monks, Eanzan and Tekido, were walking along a muddy road when they came upon a beautiful woman unable to cross the road without getting her silk shoes muddy. Without saying a word, Eanzan picked up and carried the woman across the road, leaving her on the other side. Then the two monks continued walking without talking until the end of the day. When they reached their destination, Tekido said, " You know monks are to avoid women. Why did you pick up that woman this morning?" Eanzan replied, "I left her on the side of the road this morning. Why are you at this time still carrying her?"

CREATIVITY PRINCIPLE

BE IN THE NOW

This story emphasizes the Zen philosophy that it is important to go through life not carrying around yesterday or tomorrow. Yet this is what most people in our society do. At any given time, at work or elsewhere, their minds are far, far away - mostly thinking about worries, regrets, plans, memories, or fantasies. Worrying is what much of people's thinking is about.

Fear, anxiety, and guilt are emotions that worrying encompasses. Most people are worrying about what happened yesterday or what will happen tomorrow. Worry is so rampant in North America that certain researchers claim that approximately one out of three people in North American society has serious mental problems. (As an optional exercise, the next time you are with two other people take a good look at them. If both of them look okay, it's probably you with the serious mental problems - I'm just kidding!)

Considering that we live on the continent which is still considered the land of opportunity, we have to assume that most worry is self-inflicted and somewhat useless. The following chart gives an indication of the folly of most of our worries.

WASTED WORRIES

☆ 40% of worries are about events which will never happen.

☆ 30% of worries are about events which already happened.

☆ 22% of worries are about trivial events.

☆ 4% of worries are about real events we cannot change.

☆ 4% of worries are about real events which we can act on.

The above chart indicates that 96% of the energy we spend on worrying is wasted. Some people worry so much that they worry if they do not have anything to worry about. It is no wonder they miss the moment. What are you like? Are you spending too much time worrying and missing out on today? Can you concentrate and be in the here and now? Doing the next exercise is somewhat revealing to most people.

Exercise #13-2   -   Contemplating A Paper Clip

Choose a simple object like a piece of chalk or a paper clip. Concentrate on the object for five minutes. Your task is not to let any other thoughts interfere with your thoughts about the object. In thinking about the object, think about the form as well as the concept behind the form. Where did the object come from? Who invented it? Why is its shape the way it is?

How did you do on this exercise? If you are like most people, you had trouble with wandering thoughts. You became critical, judgmental, or helpless in doing and thinking about this ridiculous excercise. Having difficulty with this exercise indicates how our thinking often is very much out of control. However, we do not have to despair. Practice can help us overcome this. We can develop the ability to be in the here and now if we want to.

The ability to experience the here and now is a characteristic of creative individuals. Highly creative people are those who can get totally immersed in a project. Their concentration level is so high that they lose all sense of time. Their project totally envelopes them. Having distracting thoughts is not a problem. Their secret? They enjoy the moment for what it is and do not worry about what is coming up next.

EXERCISES TO HELP DEVELOP PRESENCE OF MIND

Following are three exercises to help you develop your ability to be in the here and now. Individuals who have used these exercises improve their concentration level and their ability to enjoy the moment.

Exercise #13-3 - Concentrating On Better Concentration

Take an simple object and study it intently for five minutes every day. Concentrate on its form as well as the form behind it. After two or three days, when you have totally explored the first object, use another simple object. Change objects as necessary.

This exercise should be done for at least thirty straight days. The gestation period is this long because this is how long it takes for our minds to change and develop better concentration. Every time you miss a day, you should go back to square one and try for thirty days straight.

The benefits of this exercise cannot be explained in normal engineering or business-school logic. Nonetheless, the benefits are real. Your subconscious faculties will open up to enable you to concentrate in ways you haven't before.

Exercise #13-4 - Clocking Your Concentration

Have the alarm of your clock or watch go off at various times of the day to remind you to be in the here and now and enjoy the moment. Use this as a reminder to have the presence of mind to get totally immersed in what you are doing.

This can be a reminder to truly enjoy your work by doing one thing at a time. It may be a reminder to savor the taste of food by eating slowly. You may be reminded to fully experience a beautiful sunset or to be totally present with the people around you. No matter what it is, try and do what your are doing completely instead of doing it in a mediocre way while your mind is thousands of miles away.

Exercise #13-5 - Concentrating On Control of Emotions

This exercise can be practised at any time and at any place. The purpose is to concentrate on your emotional feelings, anytime they occur. Whenever, your emotions, positive or negative, are aroused, try to be aware of the reasons for them.

Ask yourself what message the feelings are conveying. Why are you feeling this way? Do your feelings have to do with worry, fear, anxiety, or guilt?

Although this exercise seems to interfere with our spontaneity, it does just the opposite. This exercise helps us get in tune with the messages from inside. In turn, we are better able to act upon what we feel without repressing any feelings. Spontaneity, which is discussed later, is actually increased when we improve our presence of mind.

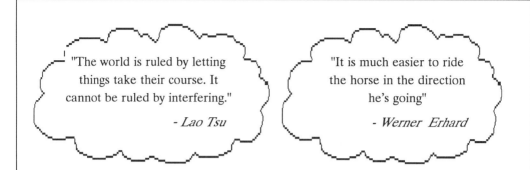

"The world is ruled by letting things take their course. It cannot be ruled by interfering."

- Lao Tsu

"It is much easier to ride the horse in the direction he's going"

- Werner Erhard

GIVING UP CONTROL TO BE IN CONTROL

Many people say they want to be in total control of their lives. They worry and are insecure when they feel out of control. The need for control can be self-defeating. The highly creative of this world tell us that one important factor in being creative is having the ability to surrender or give up the need to control. Of course this goes against what we have allowed ourselves to believe. To illustrate the importance of giving up control in life, I find it useful to use this analogy.

⇨ Assume you are on a raft floating down a fast-moving and highly-treacherous river. The raft happens to capsize and you fall into the rapidly-flowing water. There are two things you can do. One is to try and take control and fight the river. If you do this you are liable to end up injured, as a result of being thrown against the rocks. The second thing you can do is give up total control. The moment you give up control you will be in control. You are now going with the flow. The water doesn't go into the rocks. The water goes around the rocks.

Life is a fast-moving river. To get through life with a minimum of scrapes and bruises, we must learn how to go with the flow. Going with the flow means giving up control. It means surrendering to the notion that we don't know how anything is going to turn out. The best way to be in control of our destinies is to give up control and not worry about how things are going to turn. Too many factors beyond our control will destroy the best of plans.

Abraham Lincoln said "When you have got an elephant by the hind leg, and he is trying to run away, it's best to let him run". Lincoln was talking about the importance of surrendering and going with the flow. In going with the flow creative people are acknowledging that many things will not work. However, they also realize many things will work out well in the end.

Spending time worrying about past happenings or future conerns is a waste of energy. Creative people realize that Murphy's law has some bearing on the way things will be. That is "If anything can go wrong, it will." Hurdles are a certainty in the game of life. There is no way for the highly creative to eliminate all the hurdles. They accept that many will appear. However, they realize there is a way to overcome virtually all the hurdles.

When a hurdle appears, creative people will figure out a way of getting over it. If they can't get over it, they will go under it. If they can't get under it, they will go around it. If they can't go around it, they will go through it. Because of all these options, there is no need to worry about future hurdles. What is important is whether or not there is a hurdle now. If there not one, fine. If there is one, even better. Remember a problem is an opportunity. Creative people know that there is nothing but the now. What else can there be? The only thing we ever get or experience in life is the now.

ONLY INSECURE PEOPLE STRIVE FOR SECURITY

Try and answer this question honestly. How much modern-day security do you need in your life? That is how much money or how many material possessions do you think are necessary to lead a happy and fulfilling life?

Society has programmed most of us to believe that we should be preoccupied with accumulating material wealth as security for our retirement and for the unexpected events in our lives. Security is good except the people who are most preoccupied with security are the most insecure. Banks and insurance companies like people who are neurotic about the future. These are the people off whom the companies make the most money.

Materialistic and monetary security has its limits. The super rich can be killed in accidents. Their health can fail just as easily as someone with much less money. War can break out and affect the rich as well as the poor. Many rich people worry about losing their money in the event of a monetary collapse. Total security based on external possessions is an illusion.

The best form of security is internal security. This is what the word security originally referred to. Security is a derivative of the Latin word "securus" meaning "without care". A truly secure person has an internal security based on his or her creative essence. Security is the confidence to creatively handle or overcome all the situations that will happen in the future. The insecure person worries or cares about having more security. The secure person has learned how to be "without care" and not worry about security.

HOW NOT TO PREPARE IMPROMPTU SPEECHES

I think Mark Twain was probably speaking of his lack of spontaneity as an adult when he said "It usually takes me more than three weeks to prepare a good impromptu speech". Abraham Maslow, the famous humanist physchologist, believed that spontaneity is a trait which is too often lost as people grow older. Maslow said "Almost any child can compose a song or poem or a dance or a painting or a play or a game on the spur of the moment, without planning or previous intent." The majority of adults lose this ability according to Maslow.

However, Maslow found a small fraction of adults did not lose this trait and if they did, they regained it later in life. These were the people who were self-actualized. Self-actualization is a state of outstanding mental health. Maslow called this state a state of being fully human, one of moving toward maturity. He found self-actualized people to be both spontaneous and highly creative.

Spontaneity is, for all intents and purposes, synonymous with creativity. Creative people are not inhibited and are able to express their true feelings. They are able, like children, to play and act foolish. They are also able, at the spur of the moment, to decide to do something that is not in their plans for that day. Creative people also have no problem with impromptu speeches. They are more like children when they speak rather than adults.

I have found that when I do something spontaneous, then unexpected and interesting things happen to me. Many times I wind up with blockbuster ideas that I would have never got by sticking to my plans. One example is in my job as an instructor of business courses. Many of the most useful planned exercises I now use in class were discovered when I impulsively decided to try something new and unplanned.

How spontaneous are you? Do you always stick to your plans for the day? Do you always follow a set routine? How often do you decide to just forget the plans and do something different?

Exercise #13-6 - Improving Your Spontaneity

At this time I would like you to work towards being more spontaneous in your life. List some of the ways that you can be more spontaneous. Then select some of your best ones and put them in your daytimer to make sure you do them over the next few weeks.

We should all make every attempt to be more spontaneous. Spontaniety certainly opens up our creativity. Being spontaneous requires a form of strange discipline. It is a discipline that we are not used to. The discipline that is required is the ability to stray away from our plans.

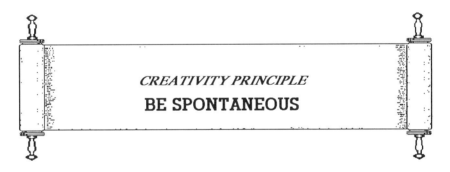

CREATIVITY PRINCIPLE

BE SPONTANEOUS

SPONTANEITY AND OXYMORONS

One final note. How did you do in Exercise #13-6? If you followed my instructions you were planning some spontaneity in your life. This does not work. Spontaneous means unplanned. "Planned spontaneity" is an oxymoron. (An oxymoron is a term for two words which are in conflict with each other. Here, for your pleasure, are some more oxymorons: little giant, dynamic inaction, professional wrestling, country music, artificial intelligence, postal service, government worker, constructive discipline and platonic relationship)

Remember to be spontaneous on a regular basis. Watch children to refresh your notion of spontaneity. Do not plan spontaneity. Be a child again.

Chapter 13 Notes

Exercises

#13-1

The Zen master revealed what he thought were the three secrets to a satisfying life.

☆ 1. Pay Attention

☆ 2. Pay Attention

☆ 3. Pay Attention

CHAPTER 14

Don't Put Off Your Procrastinating

"A story must simmer in its own juice for months or even years before it's ready to serve."

- author Edna Ferber

"Patience is a necessary ingredient of genius"

- Benjamin Disraeli

PROCRASTINATE AND BE MORE CREATIVE

One of the best ways for us to be more creative is to slow down and take our time in doing some tasks. We can actually be more productive by slowing down. Even procrastinating has its merits. By putting things off, we can be more efficient. This chapter is, in part, about the art of procrastination.

Attempt the following exercise to test your creativity.

Exercise #14-1 - Twice As Fishy But Just As Square

Mrs Colleen Waller, a wealthy businesswoman, had a lovely square fishpond on her Toronto estate. On each corner of the fishpond was a round lily pond, as shown below. Mrs Waller wanted to double the size of her fishpond to accomodate twice as many fish; however, she did not want to disturb her four lily ponds. Colleen wanted to keep the fish pond square. The lily ponds were required to be outside the perimeter of the fish pond.

She spoke to her gardener about this. He said it was impossible and all four lily ponds would have to be moved. How many lily ponds would you move?

Allow yourself 30 seconds to complete this problem.

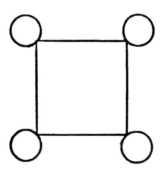

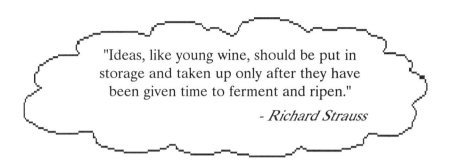

"Ideas, like young wine, should be put in storage and taken up only after they have been given time to ferment and ripen."

- Richard Strauss

What solution did you arrive at? Did you come to the conclusion that at least one lily pond did not have to be moved? Optimally, no lily ponds have to be moved. There is a solution that makes this possible (see chapter notes). Did you get this solution? If not, why not? You probably didn't get this better solution because I didn't allow you enough time. More time would have given you more opportunity to "see the light"..

Not taking enough time with a problem is something most of us do too often. In doing so, we wind up with solutions which are at worst, totally unworkable, and at best, lacking in effectiveness. We must discipline ourselves to avoid rushing through situations when we can afford extra time for generating ideas. Sufficient time should be give for the generation of a large number of solutions. This necessitates delayed decision making.

Delaying action on problems can be very important for generating highly-creative solutions. Too often, we rush solving a problem when we would be better off to wait. Many problems and situations are not as urgent as we make them out to be. When they aren't, it's best for us to take the time to let our minds play with the problem. Then our minds can report back at a later day.

Exercise #14-2 - Can You Remember Back When?

Assume that you have been given the task of planning a class reunion for all your classmates from grade 1 to grade 4. How many names can you think of in the next five minutes?

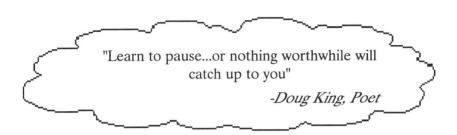

"Learn to pause...or nothing worthwhile will catch up to you"

-*Doug King, Poet*

How many did you get? Ten to twenty? How many classmates did you have in those four years? Some of them moved. Some new ones joined your class over that period. You probably have missed naming a number of them. If you are given the rest of the day to think of all of them, you will undoubtedly get more names. Names will even come to you when you are thinking about something else. At the end of the day you may have thought of 60% of the classmates that you had.

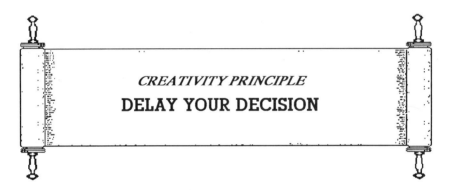

CREATIVITY PRINCIPLE

DELAY YOUR DECISION

Then tomorrow you will think of more names if you are still focusing on this task. Of course, again some names will come to you while thinking about other things. Eventually after two or three days, you will have remembered most of your classmates from those years.

Giving time for incubation of ideas works in much the same way as trying to think of your classmates' names over a long time period. Your subconscious mind is given a chance to generate more ideas than if you consciously try to come up with all available solutions in a short period of time. Sudden ideas generated in a limited time span tend to be the product of structured and rational thinking processes. Incubation over a long period of time overcomes the constraints of short-term decision making.

Try the following exercise allowing yourself two minutes.

Exercise #14-3 - Breaking The Chain Of Demand

A wealthy businessman and his chauffeur are robbed on their way to the city by a group of modern-day bandits. Their limousine and nearly all of their possessions are stolen. All the businessman has left that is valuable is a gold chain with 23 links. The businessman is too old to walk long distances. He finds the nearest hotel and sends his chauffeur for money and a new car. The chauffeur will take 23 days to fetch a car and some money and return. The hotel owner demands that the businessman give him one gold link each day as security for future payment. The businessman does not want to give the hotel owner more links than the number of nights he has stayed at the hotel. He wants to recover his chain with the fewest possible links that have been cut. What must the businessman do to give the hotel owner one link a day but cut as few links as possible?

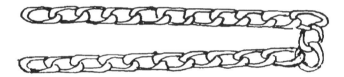

If you did what most people do with the above exercise, you determined that every second link had to be cut. This gives the minimum number cut as 11. Actually there is a better solution with a lower number of required cuts. If you take your time and approach this problem from other perspectives you may see the optimum solution. Try it. We'll come back to this later.

Incubation involves putting the problem on the back burner. This allows us to attend to other matters while the problem simmers away in our sub-conscious. We get away from direct involvement with the problem. In this way we suspend judgment and allow ourselves the luxury of having the problem travel through our various states of minds. In time we will have had several solutions come and go at unexpected times. Because these solutions will just pop out of nowhere, it is important that we write them down. Otherwise we stand the chance of forgetting some excellent solutions.

"Your Honour, the jury members request the rest of the summer to think about it."

Allowing more time results in our experiencing greater perception. Associations with other stimulants generate new perspectives which we do not experience when we rush through the problem. We avoid the rigidity that we have in the initial stages. This results in new and more open observations which lead to interesting and sometimes stunning ideas.

In solving Exercise #14-3, you can just accept that 11 links have to be cut. However, if you decide to take more time, you likely will get a better solution. If you put this problem on the back burner of your mind, tomorrow or another day the solution can hit you out of nowhere. Suppose you are in a store paying for a $2.00 item with a $5.00 bill. The clerk gives you $3.00 (in $1 bills) back. An association of this transaction can be made to the problem of the businessman with the gold chain. Where may this lead?

At this point it may occur to you that this type of transaction can be made by the businessman and the hotel owner, only it will be with gold links and not dollars. (Hint: On a particular day, does the businessman have to deal with a denomination of only 1 gold link? Can't he give a higher denomination, say 3 links together, and get change, 2 single links, back? Where will this thinking lead to? Now play around with the problem for a better solution. The optimum solution to the problem is that only two links have to be cut. See if you can figure out which two links these are.

For most problems, various associations with unrelated items can be made during the incubation stage. This may lead to several good answers. A new problem may also arise. The problem may be that of choosing the best answer from the many outstanding ones you have generated. This is a good problem to have.

IDEATING STUNNING SOLUTIONS

Disciplining yourself to avoid rushing through a problem is the first step in finding stunning or organismic solutions. This requires the presence of mind to convince yourself that the world is not going to come to an end if you do not make a decision today. Some problem-solving is urgent; some is not. Once you have decided that you have the luxury of additional time, you are well on your way to finding a better answer. We saw how taking time with Exercise #14-3 can lead to a much better solution than we had originally thought possible. (the solution is that we have to cut only the fourth and eleventh link in the chain.)

Looking for better solutions can be done consciously by stating the problem to yourself for several days. Reminding yourself of the problem can be done in many ways. Here are some of the ways to consciously attend to the problem in preparation for letting your subconscious mind do the work to find a blockbuster solution.

☆ Write your problem on several strips of paper. Leave these strips in various locations so that you come across them from time to time. Leave one in your briefcase, one in the medicine cabinet, one on the car dash, one on your office desk, and so on. In this way you will be reminded about your problem unexpectedly.

☆ Remind yourself of the problem while performing physical activities. Do this while walking, exercising, cleaning the house, or shovelling the walk. Whisper your problem while shaving or putting your make-up on.

☆ State your problem while meditating in private, daydreaming in your office, or resting on the sofa.

☆ State your problem to yourself the first thing in the morning after you get up. State it a second time and then leave it alone for awhile.

It is important to note that you are not being asked to worry about your problem day and night. You are to consciously think about the problem at the various times with full confidence that an answer will appear in due time.

After several days of consciously thinking about your problem, the stunning answer may have appeared. If it has, the mission is complete. If it hasn't, then stop thinking about the problem consciously. Allow the problem to simmer in your sub-conscious for some time after. Seemingly, out of nowhere, answers will appear. Eventually, one will surface with a stunning effect. Eureka! Intuitively you will know that this is the great one.

Chapter 14 Notes

Exercises

#14-1

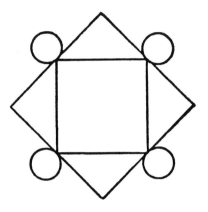

#14-2

How am I supposed to know who you went to school with? I can't even remember half of the people I went to school with.

#14-3

Read the chapter fully. The solution is stated in the content.

CHAPTER 15

The End Has Just Begun

"Everyone who's ever taken a shower has had an idea. It's the person who gets out of the shower, dries off, and does something about it who makes a difference"

- Nolan Bushell, founder of Atari

"If at first you don't succeed, you're running about average."

- Anon

To Know And Not To Do Is Not Yet To Know

- Buddist Saying

MOTIVATION JUNKIES ARE NOT MOTIVATED

I am amazed by the number of people I have encountered during my travels who go to all sorts of inspirational seminars, listen to countless cassette tapes, and read the latest "how to" books but still never get around to accomplishing anything of major importance. Many of these seminar, tape, and book "junkies" spend a lot of time telling others what it takes to be successful. Unfortunately they never quite get around to succeeding at much themselves.

Another thing that amazes me is the number of people who want to hear "motivational" speakers at dinner meetings and conferences. I occassionally get asked whether I can provide seminars and speeches that are highly motivational. It is then that I assume I will be talking to many unmotivated people. The point is that people who constantly need to be motivated in life are essentially not motivated. People who are truly internally motivated don't have to go around looking for someone to motivate them.

The doers of this world are people who know what it takes to be successful. They realize that success and accomplishment cannot come only from the knowledge of success techniques. With knowledge there has to be action. Only through effort and activity can creative and innovative projects be accomplished. The Buddists say "To know and not to do is not yet to know". It is one thing to know and recite principles and techniques. It is another thing to live these principles and put the techniques to good use. Once we have acquired the knowledge, our work has just begun.

INSTANT SUCCESS MAY TAKE MANY YEARS

I often hear that self-improvement books are a rip-off because they do not help anyone. A friend of mine tried to convince me that the only people who benefit from success books are the people who write the books. Her statement was based on the premise that success books are written for the main purpose of making money for the authors. She somehow concluded that these books did not have any value because of the profit motive. I then suggested to her that based on her logic her work at her job did not have any value since she was doing it for the primary purpose of making money.

THE INSTANT SUCCESS MANUAL FOR MOTIVATION JUNKIES

HOW YOU CAN MAKE 12 TRILLION DOLLARS IN JUST TWO DAYS BY TAKING IT EASY

By I.M. Lying

People who read "success" or "how to" books and never benefit from them are those who are looking for the quick fix. My "Easy Rule Of Life" from Chapter 3 applies here. These people are looking for the easy way out. The expectation is to read a success book and become a success overnight. They want the books to make them successful without any effort from themselves.

The idea of easy and instant success is ridiculous simply because all worthwhile success comes from hard work over a period of several years. To have an easy life we must do the difficult and uncomfortable. There is work involved in applying the principles and techniques that we read about in books. This book is no different from all other self-improvement books. It stands a chance of helping only those who help themselves by putting in a great deal of effort over a long period of time.

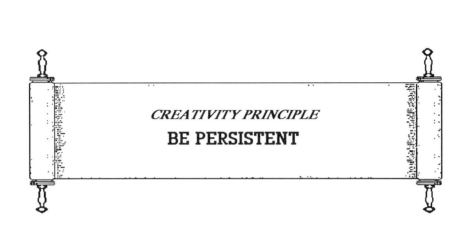

CREATIVITY PRINCIPLE

BE PERSISTENT

UNCERTAINTY, PERSISTENCE, AND YOU IN THE NEW BUSINESS WORLD

In the preceeding chapters, we looked at principles which I consider vital for our creative success. These are principles that, if followed regularly, can make a big difference in our lives. Even by using these principles infrequently, we have a chance to impact substantially upon our lives and those of others.

The question is "Is our success in business assured if we follow all the creativity principles." Before I answer that, first let us look at the business world as it looks today. Following are the conditions that reflect the modern business world. This is the climate that everyone of us has to deal with. We have virtually no choice about whether or not we can escape these business conditions.

- ✓ Intense and accelerating change
- ✓ Unpredictable
- ✓ Unstable to a point of being chaotic
- ✓ Impact of high technology
- ✓ Service-oriented economy
- ✓ Powerful consumer forces
- ✓ Global economy

The end result of these conditions is that no organization nor person can take anything for granted. There is but one certainty in today's business world. **The only certainty is uncertainty.** This is one thing we can count on. Beyond this there are no guarantees.

Even if we follow all the creativity principles, our success is not always certain. Then why should we follow and apply these principles and techniques? Simply because our chances for creative success are increased by at least 10000 times when we persist in following these principles. Increasing our odds by this much makes it all worthwhile. Being persistent in being creative will have its payoffs on most, if not all, projects we undertake.

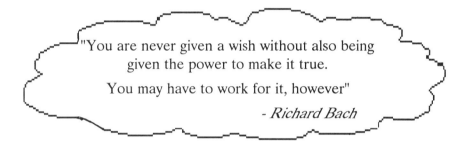

"You are never given a wish without also being
given the power to make it true.

You may have to work for it, however"

- Richard Bach

The business world of the 1990's and beyond will be frustrating and unrewarding for those who choose not to use their creative abilites. For those who develop their creative skills and persist in using them, the times will offer many opportunities. People who have learned to think laterally, search for many solutions, look for the obvious, take risks, celebrate failure, fully explore all ideas, and like chaos will be the ones who are at the forefront of business. They will be the people making a difference as entrepreneurs in their own businesses or as leaders of the progressive companies of the new world.

The question you should ask yourself is "Do I want to make a creative difference in this new world?" Once you have decided you do, you must be committed to making that difference. You are the only person who can choose for you to be creative. You are the only person who can do the work that needs to be done. You are the only person who can supply the energy, the enthusiasm, the courage, the unreasonableness, the spontaneity, the discipline, and the persistence that is required. The world of business and your personal life will be as adventurous, exciting, and rewarding as you want them to be.

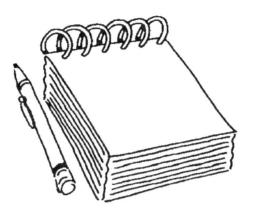

Comments Or Questions?

I hope you enjoyed *"The Art Of Seeing Double Or Better In Business"*. If you have any comments or questions, I will be pleased to hear from you. Please send all correspondence to Zelinski Multi-Vision Learning, 10518-68 Ave., Edmonton, Alberta, Canada, T5H 2B1.

CUSTOM-DESIGNED PRESENTATIONS
FOR YOUR SPECIAL EVENT

Let Ernie Zelinski custom design a seminar or speech on creativity and innovation for your next convention, meeting, management retreat, or company sponsored cruise. Your input will ensure that the tailor-made presentation is what you want.

You get to choose the topics to be covered as well as the length of the presentation. A program can be designed to take anywhere from less than an hour to two or more days.

The program will be a lively and interesting session made more enjoyable through audience participation, group exercises, and case studies.

You can book the presentation you want by contacting:

Zelinski Multi-Vision Learning
10518-68 Ave.
Edmonton, Alberta
T6H 2B1
Phone (403) 434-9202

Can*Speak Presentations Ltd.
#104, 1260 Hornby Street
Vancouver, B.C.
V6Z 1W2
Phone (604) 687-6868